Scholastic
Children's Guide to Dinosaurs
and Other
Prehistoric Animals

Quetzalcoatlus

Previous page: *Dilophosaurus*
Facing page: *Saltopus*

Scholastic
Children's Guide to Dinosaurs
and Other
Prehistoric Animals

PHILIP WHITFIELD

Scholastic Canada Ltd.

A Marshall Edition
This book was conceived, edited and designed by
Marshall Editions
170 Piccadilly, London W1V 9DD

Scholastic Canada Ltd.
123 Newkirk Road
Richmond Hill, Ontario L4C 3G5

First Canadian edition
10 9 8 7 6 5 4 3 2 1

Canadian Cataloguing in Publication Data

Whitfield, Philip
    Scholastic children's guide to dinosaurs
and other prehistoric animals

Canadian Ed.
Includes index.
ISBN 0–590=24329–2

1. Dinosaurs – Encyclopedias, Juvenile.
2. Animals, Fossils – Encyclopedias, Juvenile.
3. Paleontology – Encyclopedias, Juvenile.
I. Title.

QE862.D5W55 1994 j567.9'1'03 C94–930675–4

Film supplied by Dorchester Typesetting Group
Limited
Origination by Chroma Graphics, Singapore

Printed in EEC, Officine Grafiche De Agostini - Novara 1994
Bound by Legatoria del Verbano S.p.A.

CONTENTS

Torosaurus

Elasmosaurus

INTRODUCTION

Once, dinosaurs were living, breathing creatures—not just models or fossils in museums. They, and the other animals of their time, moved, ate, and even took care of their babies. The aim of this book is to bring dinosaurs and other prehistoric animals to life again, to describe how they might have looked and behaved.

The following chapters cover the periods when dinosaurs flourished—the Triassic, Jurassic and Cretaceous. The Jurassic and Cretaceous, when most dinosaurs lived, are further split into two chapters—making five chapters in all.

Each chapter begins with a spectacular artist's reconstruction of life at that time. While this can only be an idea, not fact, it is not fantasy and provides a visual impression of the prehistoric world. This illustration is fully explained on the following pages and a world map shows the positions of the continents at that time, which were different from those of today.

Illustrated "catalogues" of dinosaurs and other reptiles of each period follow. The group name and size of each are given and a

Key to silhouettes

Silhouette used for animals
more than 1 metre long

Silhouette used for animals
1 metre long and under

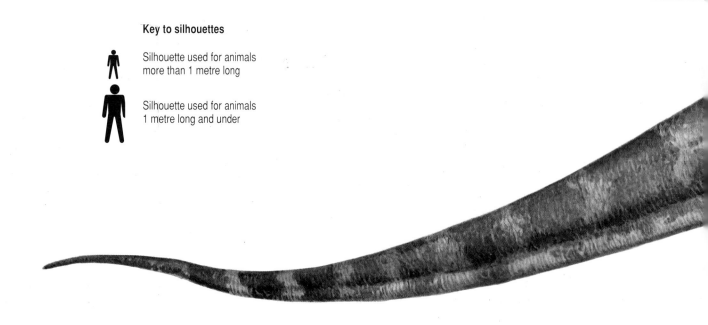

silhouette compares the size of each to that of an adult human. Each catalogue page features the animals of a particular area—North America, Africa, Europe, Asia and so on. These areas are where fossils of the animals have been found—they may well have ranged further when alive. And, of course, what is called Africa today, for example, may not have been in the same position then. There are more pages on the animals of North America and Europe because more fossils have been found there than in other areas.

Within each chapter, special "Focus on" features look at one particular creature or group of creatures in more detail—pterosaurs, stegosaurs and tyrannosaurs, for example. These pages explore the varying lifestyles of these fascinating creatures.

A few mammals, amphibians and other creatures do appear in the panorama scenes, but this book is mostly about the dinosaurs and other reptiles. The Triassic, Jurassic and Cretaceous periods were the age of the reptiles, the time when some of the largest and most extraordinary animals that ever existed ruled the Earth.

Tenontosaurus

The age of the dinosaurs

Dinosaurs were the most successful animals that have ever lived on Earth. These amazing creatures ruled the planet for about 140 million years until they mysteriously died out about 65 million years ago. While they were masters of the land, the flying pterosaurs ruled the skies and crocodiles, ichthyosaurs and plesiosaurs dominated the rivers and oceans.

Successful reptiles

Dinosaurs were reptiles. They had skeletons like those of reptiles and the same scaly skin. There were probably about 400 different kinds of dinosaurs, from gigantic creatures plodding along on all fours down to agile, fast-running bird-like animals. There were meat-eaters (carnivores) and plant-eaters (herbivores), as well as omnivores that tackled more or less anything.

Lizard-hipped and bird-hipped

Scientists divide the dinosaurs into two main groups—the lizard-hipped and the bird-hipped—according to the design of their skeletons. As the names suggest, the important differences have to do with the structure of the hip bones. Both groups, though, included dinosaurs that walked on two legs and dinosaurs that walked on all fours.

In the lizard-hipped dinosaurs, the two lower hip bones point in opposite directions, just as they do in lizards. But in the bird-hipped dinosaurs, the lower hip bones are long and thin, and point backwards, as they do in today's birds.

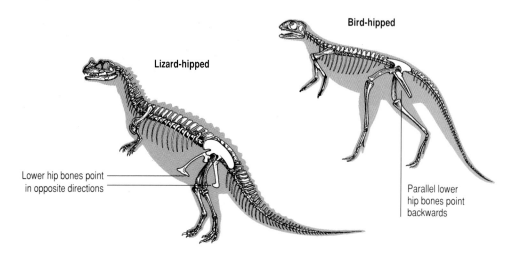

Bird-hipped

Lizard-hipped

Lower hip bones point in opposite directions

Parallel lower hip bones point backwards

Spinosaurus was a large carnivorous dinosaur that lived in Africa in the Late Cretaceous period.

Prehistoric reptiles
While the dinosaurs were the dominant land animals during the Triassic, Jurassic and Cretaceous periods, there were many other kinds of reptiles. Here are some of the most important of the groups that appear in the following pages.

Placodont
(marine reptile)

Therapsid
(mammal-like reptile)

Ichthyosaur
(marine reptile)

Pterosaur
(flying reptile)

Crocodylian
(crocodile)

Nothosaur
(marine reptile)

Plesiosaur
(marine reptile)

Dinosaurs and their relatives

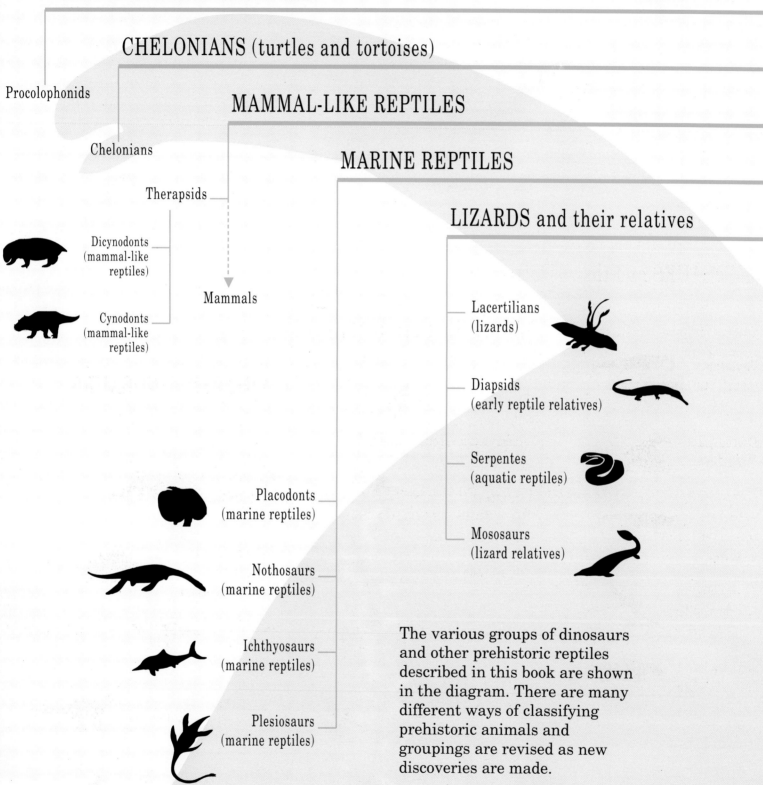

PRIMITIVE EARLY REPTILES

CHELONIANS (turtles and tortoises)

MAMMAL-LIKE REPTILES

MARINE REPTILES

Procolophonids

Chelonians

Therapsids

LIZARDS and their relatives

Dicynodonts
(mammal-like
reptiles)

Cynodonts
(mammal-like
reptiles)

Mammals

Lacertilians
(lizards)

Diapsids
(early reptile relatives)

Serpentes
(aquatic reptiles)

Mososaurs
(lizard relatives)

Placodonts
(marine reptiles)

Nothosaurs
(marine reptiles)

Ichthyosaurs
(marine reptiles)

Plesiosaurs
(marine reptiles)

The various groups of dinosaurs
and other prehistoric reptiles
described in this book are shown
in the diagram. There are many
different ways of classifying
prehistoric animals and
groupings are revised as new
discoveries are made.

ARCHOSAURS and their relatives

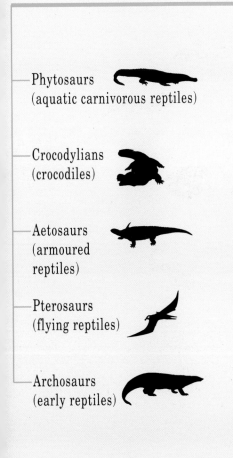

- Phytosaurs
  (aquatic carnivorous reptiles)

- Crocodylians
  (crocodiles)

- Aetosaurs
  (armoured
  reptiles)

- Pterosaurs
  (flying reptiles)

- Archosaurs
  (early reptiles)

LIZARD-HIPPED DINOSAURS

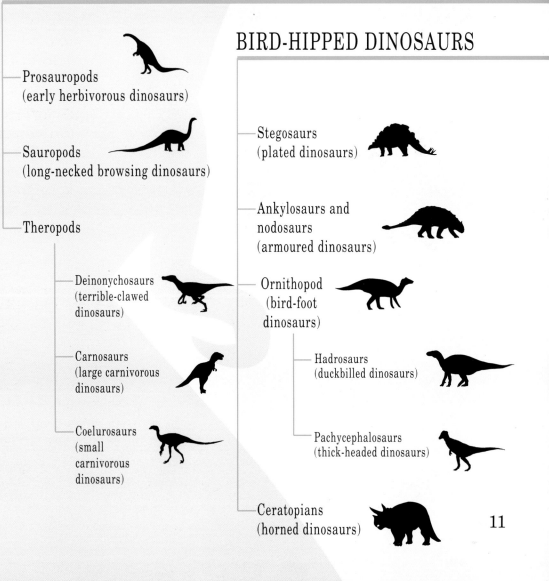

- Prosauropods
  (early herbivorous dinosaurs)

- Sauropods
  (long-necked browsing dinosaurs)

- Theropods

  - Deinonychosaurs
    (terrible-clawed
    dinosaurs)

  - Carnosaurs
    (large carnivorous
    dinosaurs)

  - Coelurosaurs
    (small
    carnivorous
    dinosaurs)

BIRD-HIPPED DINOSAURS

- Stegosaurs
  (plated dinosaurs)

- Ankylosaurs and
  nodosaurs
  (armoured dinosaurs)

- Ornithopod
  (bird-foot
  dinosaurs)

  - Hadrosaurs
    (duckbilled dinosaurs)

  - Pachycephalosaurs
    (thick-headed dinosaurs)

- Ceratopians
  (horned dinosaurs)

11

Desmatosuchus   Henodus   Nothosaurus   Cynognathus   Lystrosaurus

Life in the Triassic

About 200 million years ago, in the middle of Triassic times, the earliest dinosaurs were walking the Earth. At this time most of the land was joined together and dinosaurs and other animals could roam overland to almost anywhere in the world.

Planet Earth was much drier in the Triassic than it is now, and there were large deserts in inland areas. There were no flowering plants or grasses—they evolved much later. The most common trees were conifers, similar to today's pines. Other large plants included yews, ginkgos and the palm-like cycads. Moisture-loving ferns and horsetails thrived by lakes and rivers.

The first dinosaurs shared the Earth with other reptiles, such as lizards and crocodiles, and with amphibians. There were many insects, too, some similar to those of today, such as beetles, grasshoppers and cockroaches. And flies, bees and wasps first evolved during the Triassic period.

14

A drying lake in North America

Long-necked *Massospondylus* was one of the first tall plant-eating dinosaurs ever to live on Earth.

Coelophysis was a fierce, fast-moving hunter. It ran on two legs, leaving its sharp-clawed hands free for grasping prey. Scientists believe that by hunting in packs, *Coelophysis* could probably overcome prey larger than themselves.

There was a greater area of desert in North America in Triassic times. Plants tended to grow around lakes or temporary pools of water formed after rains. This panorama shows the animal and plant life surrounding a drying lake.

Massospondylus

Riojasaurus

Procompsognathus

Saltopus

Plateosaurus

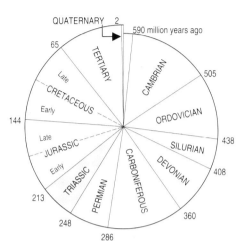

Ferns and tree ferns, which first evolved about 400 million years ago, were an important food for the first plant-eating dinosaurs.

Cone-bearing cycads (seed ferns) were also common in Triassic times.

Trilophosaurus was a strongly built reptile, with a toothless beak. It fed on plants.

Metoposaurus was a large amphibian, nearly 3 metres long. It hunted other creatures for food.

The Triassic period lasted about 35 million years. It is named Triassic from the Latin word *trias,* meaning three, because European rocks of that time can be divided into three groups of different ages.

This map of the world in the Triassic period shows how most of the land made one supercontinent, known as Pangaea.

The world 240 million years ago

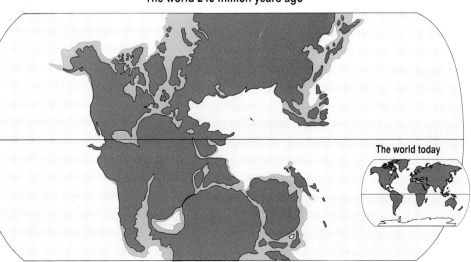

The world today

☐ SEA
◻ CONTINENTAL SHELF
■ LAND

...hrosuchus

...lky animal with short, strong legs and a large
...ead, *Erythrosuchus* was one of the largest
land-living predators in Early Triassic
times. It hunted other reptiles which it
seized in powerful jaws lined with
sharp teeth.

SIZE:
4.5 m long

GROUP:
**Archosaur
(early reptile)**

*P*lacodus

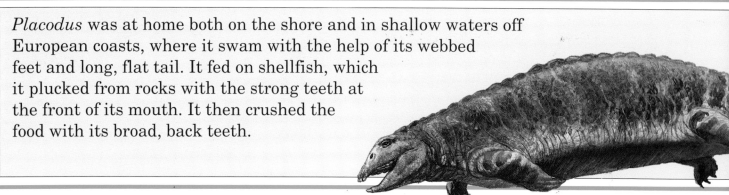

Placodus was at home both on the shore and in shallow waters off
European coasts, where it swam with the help of its webbed
feet and long, flat tail. It fed on shellfish, which
it plucked from rocks with the strong teeth at
the front of its mouth. It then crushed the
food with its broad, back teeth.

*C*hasmatosaurus

SIZE:
2 m long
GROUP:
**Archosaur
(early reptile}**

This reptile may have lived much like a
modern crocodile. It could have moved on
land but probably swam well with the
help of its long tail and may have spent
most of its life in rivers hunting fish
to eat. Its jaws were well equipped with
sharp curving teeth for seizing its prey.

*L*ystrosaurus

This sturdy plant-eating animal lived in Africa and Asia and its remains were also found in Antarctica in the late 1960s. This wide distribution is one of the many pieces of evidence that, during the Triassic period, India and all the southern continents were joined as one landmass (see map on page 15).

SIZE:
2 m long

GROUP:
Placodont (marine reptile)

SIZE:
1 m long

GROUP:
Dicynodont (mammal-like reptile)

*C*ynognathus

Strongly built and chunky, *Cynognathus* was a fierce hunter that lived in Africa. It had a large head with very sharp teeth and strong jaws, giving it tremendous biting ability.

SIZE:
1 m long

GROUP:
Cynodont (mammal-like reptile)

17

Pistosaurus

Pistosaurus had limbs shaped like paddles which helped give it its swimming ability. This streamlined reptile probably spent most of its life at sea.

It had long, narrow jaws with plenty of sharp, pointed teeth— ideal for catching fish.

Ticinosuchus

With its long, slender body, armoured with bony plates on the back and tail, *Ticinosuchus* looked a bit like a long-legged crocodile. It lived on land and hunted other creatures to eat.

Placochelys

This small reptile was well suited to life in water. It had a broad, flat, turtle-like body, protected by hard, knobby plates, and long limbs which worked as swimming paddles. *Placochelys* probably fed mainly on shellfish which it picked off rocks with its strong beak.

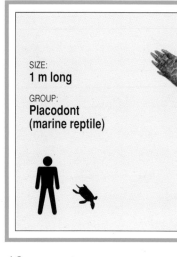

SIZE:
1 m long

GROUP:
Placodont (marine reptile)

Lariosaurus

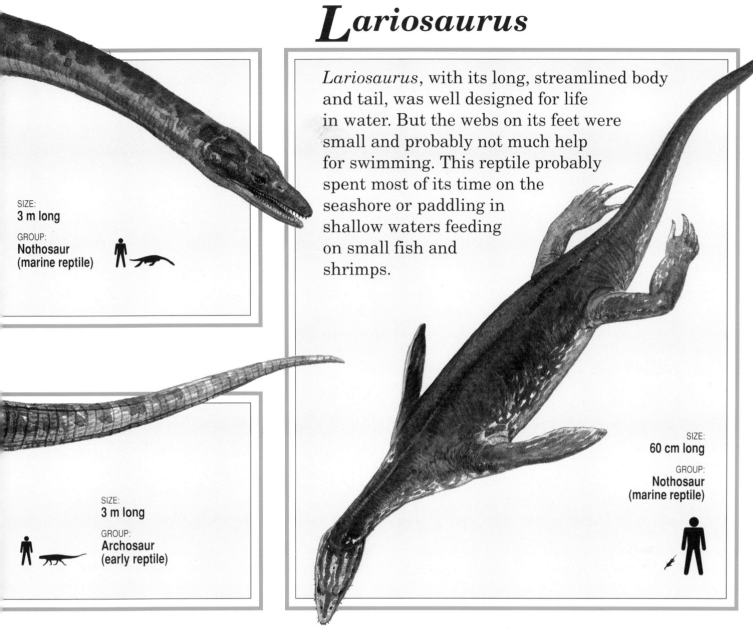

SIZE:
3 m long

GROUP:
**Nothosaur
(marine reptile)**

SIZE:
3 m long

GROUP:
**Archosaur
(early reptile)**

Lariosaurus, with its long, streamlined body and tail, was well designed for life in water. But the webs on its feet were small and probably not much help for swimming. This reptile probably spent most of its time on the seashore or paddling in shallow waters feeding on small fish and shrimps.

SIZE:
60 cm long

GROUP:
**Nothosaur
(marine reptile)**

Askeptosaurus

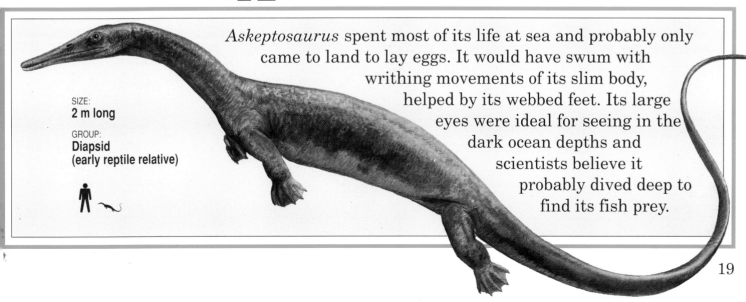

SIZE:
2 m long

GROUP:
**Diapsid
(early reptile relative)**

Askeptosaurus spent most of its life at sea and probably only came to land to lay eggs. It would have swum with writhing movements of its slim body, helped by its webbed feet. Its large eyes were ideal for seeing in the dark ocean depths and scientists believe it probably dived deep to find its fish prey.

Lagosuchus

This little reptile may have been a close relative of the mighty dinosaurs and, possibly, the pterosaurs. Scientists have discovered that the structure of its hip and leg bones closely resembles that of the dinosaurs. Although it was only about the size of a rabbit, *Lagosuchus* was a skilled hunter and seized prey in its long-fingered hands.

SIZE:
30 cm long

GROUP:
Archosaur (early reptile)

Gracilisuchus

This early type of crocodile lived on land and could run fast on its long back legs, holding its tail out to help keep its balance. It probably chased after small lizards, catching them in its strong jaws.

SIZE:
30 cm long

GROUP:
Crocodylian (crocodile)

Massetognathus

Although it was a reptile, *Massetognathus* looked much more like a mammal and may even have been covered with hair. It was a plant-eater and had very strong teeth for chewing tough leaves and stems.

SIZE:
48 cm long

GROUP:
Cynodont (mammal-like reptile)

20

Mixosaurus

A sleek fish-like creature, *Mixosaurus* had a fin on its back and paddle-shaped limbs. Like other marine reptiles, it cruised the open seas, catching and eating fish.

SIZE:
1 m long

GROUP:
Ichthyosaur (marine reptile)

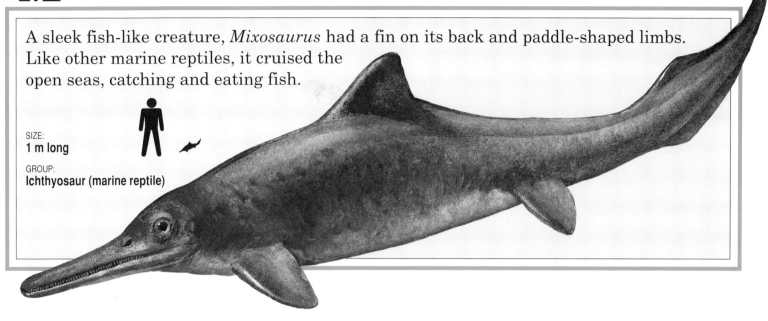

Cymbospondylus

SIZE:
10 m long

GROUP:
Ichthyosaur (marine reptile)

With no fins on its back and tail, *Cymbospondylus* looked less like a fish than many ichthyosaurs. But it did have limbs shaped like paddles, which were probably used to help steer its long body as it swam. It spent its whole life in the water, even giving birth to its young at sea. Fish were its main food, which it caught with its long, beak-like jaws equipped with sharp teeth.

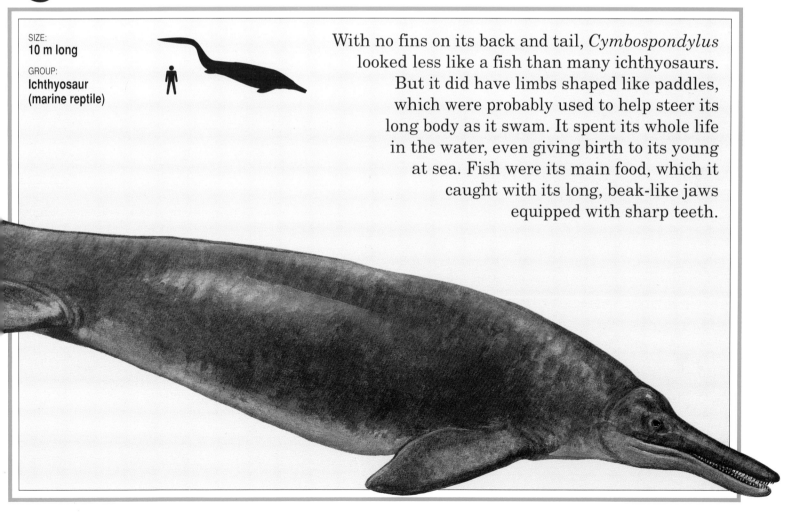

Focus on: MAMMAL-LIKE REPTILES
the ancestors of mammals

All of today's mammals—whether elephants, tigers or rats—are descended from these strange creatures, the mammal-like reptiles that dominated the world in Triassic times. The scientific name for these animals is therapsids.

They lived at the same time as ordinary reptiles but had certain very important differences. Their jaws were stronger than those of other reptiles and they had teeth of different sizes and shapes for cutting, tearing and chewing—just as mammals have today.

Two of the most successful groups of mammal-like reptiles, or therapsids, were dicynodonts, such as the bulky *Kannemeyeria,* and the cynodonts, such as *Thrinaxodon.* Both became extinct during the Triassic, but not before they had left behind them the ancestors of the modern world's most important group of animals—the mammals.

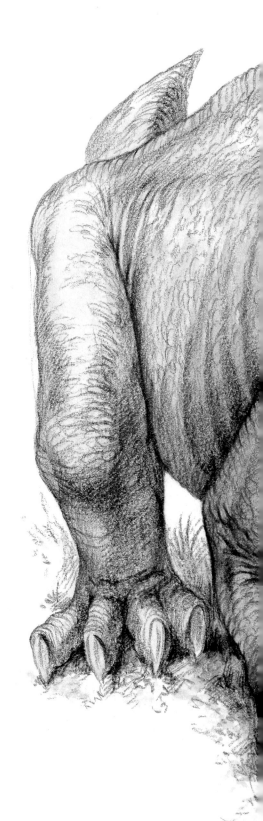

Kannemeyeria was a large, heavy-bodied creature, about 3 metres long. It fed on leaves and roots which it tore up in great mouthfuls with its strong horny beak. Fossil remains of this animal have been found in Africa, Asia and South America.

Small and solidly built, *Thrinaxodon* hunted other animals for food. It had strong legs, so could probably run after its prey quite swiftly, and powerful, mammal-like jaws. It may even have been covered with hair. *Thrinaxodon* was about 50 centimetres long and lived in Africa.

With the aid of its small teeth and agile body, *Ericiolacerta* probably fed on insects which it snapped from the air. This little reptile was only 20 centimetres long and lived in Africa about 200 million years ago.

Stagonolepis

Its bulky body and short legs made *Stagonolepis* look like a crocodile. In fact, it lived on land and fed on tough-leaved plants such as horsetails, ferns and cycads. It was a slow-moving animal, but the heavy bony plates covering its body protected it from predators.

SIZE:
3 m long

GROUP:
Archosaur (early reptile)

Eudimorphodon

Like all flying reptiles, *Eudimorphodon* had wings made of skin. These stretched between its front and back limbs and along the enormously long fourth finger of each hand. Flapping these wings, *Eudimorphodon* probably flew low over the sea, its large eyes trained on the surface to spot fish and flying insects. Its long tail would have been held straight out during flight to help balance the body.

SIZE:
75 cm wingspan

GROUP:
Pterosaur (flying reptile)

Kuehneosaurus

With the help of a pair of wings made of skin, this long-legged lizard could launch itself into the air and glide from tree to tree. Its wings stretched along each side of its body, between the front and back legs, and were supported by extra long ribs.

SIZE:
60 cm long

GROUP:
Lacertilian (lizard)

Henodus

Henodus looked very much like today's turtles with its broad, flat body. Its back and belly were covered with bony plates which protected it from the attacks of larger marine reptiles and other hunters in the sea. It had no teeth, but probably had a hard, horny beak which was useful both for scraping shellfish off rocks and for crushing them to eat.

SIZE:
1 m long

GROUP:
Placodont (marine reptile)

Ornithosuchus

SIZE:
4 m long

GROUP:
Archosaur (early reptile)

Ornithosuchus was not, as was once thought, an early dinosaur, although it looked like one. It belonged to the group of reptiles believed to be the ancestors of dinosaurs. A large, fierce-looking hunter, *Ornithosuchus* could probably move around on its hind legs and on all fours.

25

Plateosaurus

Early dinosaurs such as *Plateosaurus* were the first tall plant-eaters. This long-necked creature could rear up on its back legs and reach high into trees such as cycads and conifers to tear off leaves with its sharp teeth. This probably had a serious effect on trees of this time which had never before been fed on by such giants. When not feeding, the bulky-bodied *Plateosaurus* probably moved around on all fours. It lived in herds which travelled through the desert landscape of Europe, searching for new feeding grounds.

SIZE:
up to 7 m long

GROUP:
Prosauropod (early herbivorous dinosaur)

Hyperodapedon

Like all the rhynchosaurs, *Hyperodapedon* was a plant-eater with a stocky body. It had strong teeth specialized for chopping pieces off plants. It fed mostly on seed ferns, but by the end of the Triassic both these plants and the rhynchosaurs had died out.

SIZE:
1.2 m long

GROUP:
Rhynchosaur (early reptile)

26

*R*utiodon

SIZE:
3 m long

GROUP:
Phytosaur (aquatic carnivore)

With its long snout and body armoured with bony plates, *Rutiodon* looked, and probably behaved, very like today's crocodiles. Like crocodiles, it lived in rivers where it fed on fish that it caught in its sharp-toothed jaws. It probably also hunted other reptiles.

Procompsognathus

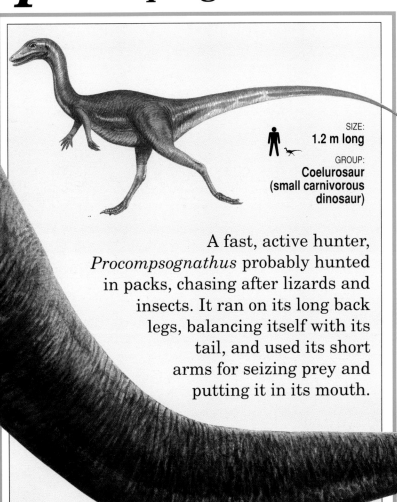

SIZE:
1.2 m long

GROUP:
Coelurosaur (small carnivorous dinosaur)

A fast, active hunter, *Procompsognathus* probably hunted in packs, chasing after lizards and insects. It ran on its long back legs, balancing itself with its tail, and used its short arms for seizing prey and putting it in its mouth.

Terrestrisuchus

The earliest crocodiles, such as *Terrestrisuchus*, spent more time on land than modern water-dwelling crocodiles. This graceful, long-legged creature was probably a fast runner and sprinted over the dry Triassic landscape snapping up insects and small lizards in its long jaws.

SIZE:
50 cm long

GROUP:
Crocodylian (crocodile)

Coelophysis

A ferocious hunter, *Coelophysis* was built for speed. Its body was light and slender and it could move fast on its long back legs. *Coelophysis* probably hunted in packs, roaming the forests in search of such prey as the small shrew-like mammals that appeared around this time.

SIZE:
3 m long

GROUP:
Coelurosaur
(small carnivorous dinosaur)

Shonisaurus

This huge creature was one of the largest in the sea in Triassic times. It had a fish-like tail, which powered its swimming, and four long, narrow paddles. Its long jaws contained teeth only at the front. Like all ichthyosaurs, *Shonisaurus* spent all its life at sea and fed on fish.

SIZE:
15 m long

GROUP:
Ichthyosaur
(marine
reptile)

28

Desmatosuchus

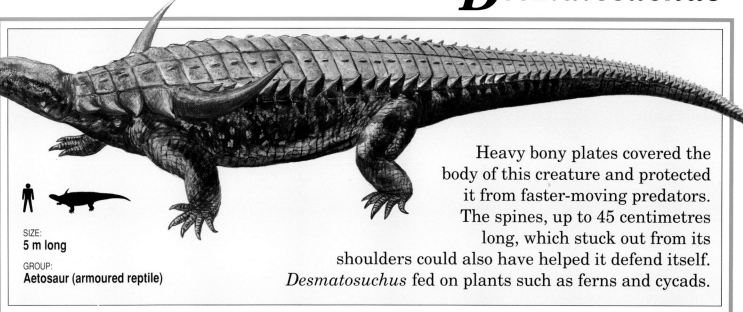

SIZE:
5 m long

GROUP:
Aetosaur (armoured reptile)

Heavy bony plates covered the body of this creature and protected it from faster-moving predators. The spines, up to 45 centimetres long, which stuck out from its shoulders could also have helped it defend itself. *Desmatosuchus* fed on plants such as ferns and cycads.

Hypsognathus

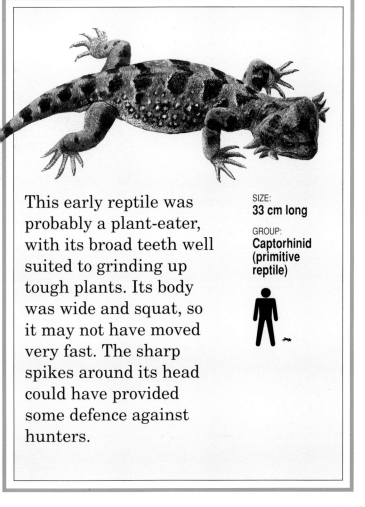

This early reptile was probably a plant-eater, with its broad teeth well suited to grinding up tough plants. Its body was wide and squat, so it may not have moved very fast. The sharp spikes around its head could have provided some defence against hunters.

SIZE:
33 cm long

GROUP:
Captorhinid (primitive reptile)

Massospondylus

Long-necked *Massospondylus* could reach high into the trees to find food. It had large hands, which it probably used for picking leaves, and each "thumb" was armed with a large, curved claw. Smooth stones have been found in the stomachs of some skeletons of this animal. It probably swallowed these to help grind up the tough plants it ate—just as some birds and crocodiles do today.

SIZE:
4 m long

GROUP:
Prosauropod (early herbivorous dinosaur)

Life in the Early Jurassic

The dry desert lands of the Triassic period had mostly disappeared by Early Jurassic times. The climate in most of the world was warm and wet.

The oceans of the world were packed with a huge range of creatures. From the sea floors sprouted graceful sea lilies or crinoids—these were not plants but many-armed relatives of starfish. Cruising through the warm waters by jerky jet propulsion were ammonites and belemnites—coiled and straight-bodied versions of today's squid and octopus.

These and other invertebrates (animals without backbones), such as molluscs, shellfish and worms, were hunted by a great variety of swimming predators. There were fish of many sorts, their bodies covered with tough heavy scales for protection.

The most powerful of all undersea hunters, however, were the huge marine reptiles such as ichthyosaurs and plesiosaurs.

Under the sea

Lepidotes was able to shape its mouth into a tube and suck prey towards it from a distance.

Ichthyosaurus had a streamlined body, shaped like a torpedo—ideal for fast swimming.

Ammonites had a squid-like body inside a coiled shell. They became extinct at the end of the Cretaceous.

Eurhinosaurus was an unusual ichthyosaur with a top jaw much longer than the lower jaw.

Dapedium had short jaws and broad teeth it may have used for crushing shellfish to eat.

Anchisaurus   Scelidosaurus   Heterodontosaurus   Scutellosaurus   Lesothosaurus

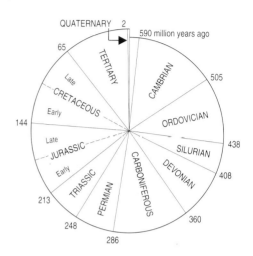

Pholidophorus was a fast-moving fish that probably hunted small shrimp-like creatures.

Temnodonto-saurus with its long, sharp-toothed jaws, was a powerful hunter. Here it is about to catch a plesiosaur.

A brittle star—these five-armed creatures still live in oceans today.

The Jurassic period began about 213 million years ago. It is named after the limestone rocks formed at this time in the sea and later thrown up as part of the Jura Mountains in Europe.

The map shows how the world might have looked in the Early Jurassic. The world's landmasses were still very close together.

Crinoids were not plants but animals that lived anchored to the seabed.

Belemnites are now extinct but probably looked much like a modern squid.

The world 210 million years ago

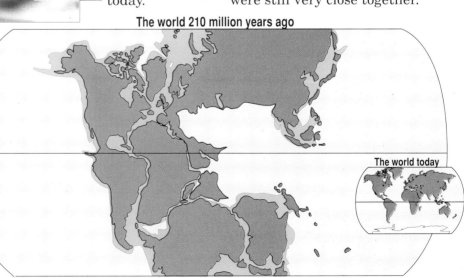

☐ SEA

▨ CONTINENTAL SHELF

▓ LAND

The world today

Teleosaurus

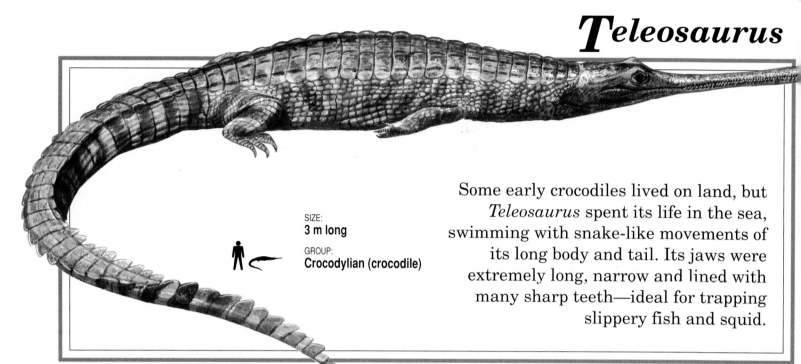

SIZE:
3 m long

GROUP:
Crocodylian (crocodile)

Some early crocodiles lived on land, but *Teleosaurus* spent its life in the sea, swimming with snake-like movements of its long body and tail. Its jaws were extremely long, narrow and lined with many sharp teeth—ideal for trapping slippery fish and squid.

Dimorphodon

Like other pterosaurs, *Dimorphodon* flew on wings that were made of skin attached to the extra long fingers of each hand. Its jaws were very unusual: large and deep, they looked like the bill of a modern puffin. Nobody knows the exact reason for this but it is possible that the deep snout was used in displays for attracting a mate or winning territory.

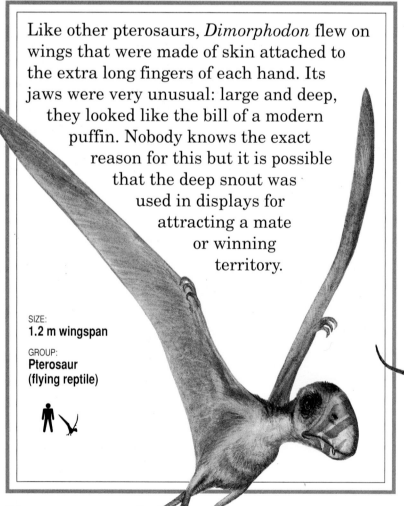

SIZE:
1.2 m wingspan

GROUP:
Pterosaur (flying reptile)

Oligokyphus

With its slender body and long tail, *Oligokyphus* was similar to a modern weasel. It may also have had hair, which would have made it look even more like a mammal. It fed on plants and had large front teeth that were good for gnawing.

SIZE:
50 cm

GROUP:
Cynodont (mammal-like reptile)

Plesiosaurus

Although not a very fast swimmer, *Plesiosaurus* was agile in the water, using its paddle-shaped flippers to turn this way and that with ease. It had a long neck which it probably stretched out to catch passing fish; it could even raise its head above the surface of the water to search for prey.

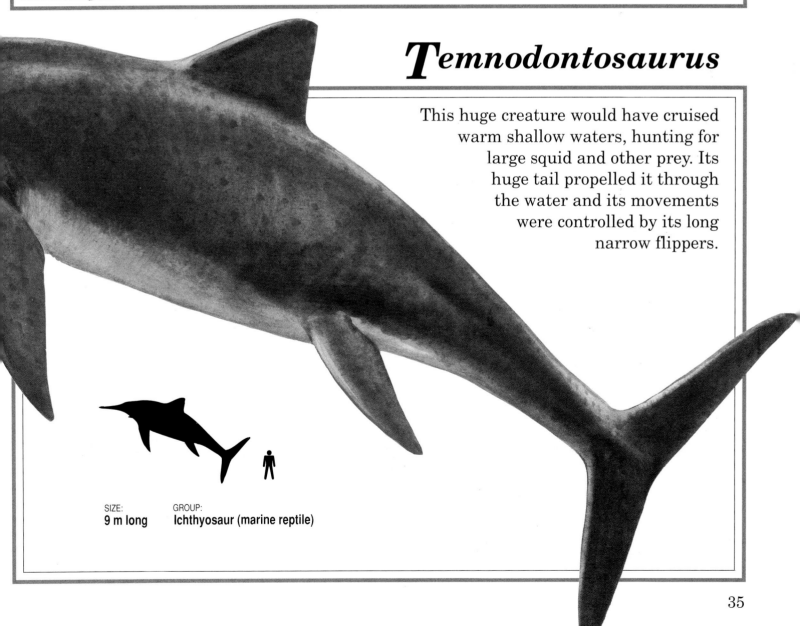

SIZE:
2.5 m long

GROUP:
**Plesiosaur
(marine reptile)**

Temnodontosaurus

This huge creature would have cruised warm shallow waters, hunting for large squid and other prey. Its huge tail propelled it through the water and its movements were controlled by its long narrow flippers.

SIZE:
9 m long

GROUP:
Ichthyosaur (marine reptile)

35

Barapasaurus

This Indian dinosaur had a huge, bulky body and thick legs like pillars—its name means "big leg lizard". It is the oldest-known long-necked dinosaur and the only one so far to have been found in India. Despite its

huge size, *Barapasaurus* was probably a gentle giant that fed on plants with the help of its saw-edged teeth.

Lesothosaurus

This small animal, which looked like a lizard, usually moved on its long back legs. It was a fast runner, well able to sprint over the hot, dry plains of its home in southern Africa. It fed on plants which it chewed with sharp, pointed teeth, shaped like little arrowheads.

SIZE:
1 m long

GROUP:
Ornithopod (bird-foot dinosaur)

Thecodontosaurus

Found in Africa and Europe, *Thecodontosaurus* was a slim creature with a small head and long neck and tail. It probably spent much of its time on all fours, feeding on low plants, but may also have stood on its hind legs to pick higher growing leaves.

SIZE:
2 m long
GROUP:
Prosauropod (early herbivorous dinosaur)

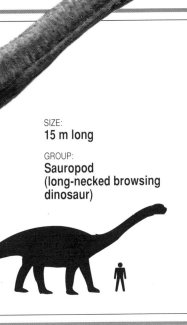

Anchisaurus

Anchisaurus lived in Africa and North America. Lightly built, it had a long neck and could stand up on its hind legs and reach high into trees to find food. On the first finger of each of its hands was a large claw which may have been used for rooting up plants or for fighting other dinosaurs.

SIZE:
15 m long

GROUP:
Sauropod (long-necked browsing dinosaur)

SIZE:
2 m long

GROUP:
Prosauropod (early herbivorous dinosaur)

Heterodontosaurus

SIZE:
1 m long

GROUP:
Ornithopod (bird-foot dinosaur)

This small African dinosaur fed on plants. It was unusual because it had three different kinds of teeth: sharp cutting teeth for biting off leaves, larger back teeth for grinding them, and some curved teeth like tusks. Nobody knows exactly what these curved ones were used for, but some experts believe that only the males had the tusks and used them as weapons when fighting.

Focus on: ICHTHYOSAURS
the swimming reptiles

Of all the marine reptiles, ichthyosaurs—whose name means "fish lizard"—were the most fully adapted to life in the sea. They even gave birth to their live young in the water, instead of laying eggs, and fossil skeletons of adults have been found with the tiny bones of babies still inside them.

Ichthyosaurs lived much like today's dolphins. They were strong swimmers and cruised the open seas of the world, feeding on fish and squid. They had a fish-like tail which moved from side to side, much as the tail of a modern shark or tuna, pushing the body through the water. At 15 metres long, *Shonisaurus* was the largest known ichthyosaur; most were smaller. *Ichthyosaurus* was 2 metres long.

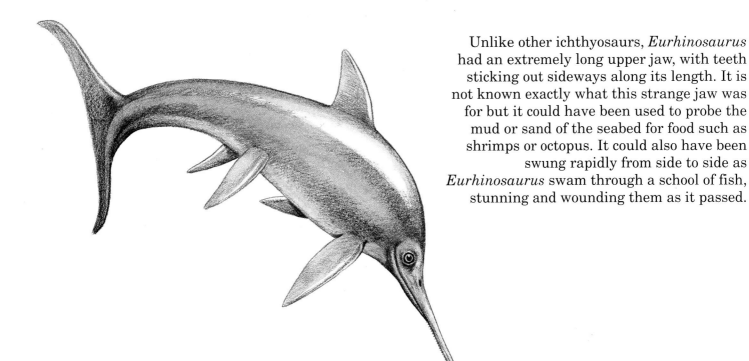

Unlike other ichthyosaurs, *Eurhinosaurus* had an extremely long upper jaw, with teeth sticking out sideways along its length. It is not known exactly what this strange jaw was for but it could have been used to probe the mud or sand of the seabed for food such as shrimps or octopus. It could also have been swung rapidly from side to side as *Eurhinosaurus* swam through a school of fish, stunning and wounding them as it passed.

Ichthyosaurus was fast and agile in the water, diving through the waves in search of prey. But although well adapted for swimming, it was still a reptile and had to come to the surface to breathe air. The nostrils were set far back on the snout near the eyes so the animal only had to raise its head to the surface of the water to take a breath.

Ichthyosaurus

Dolphin

A streamlined body, and strong tail and back fins, helped *Ichthyosaurus* swim at more than 40 kilometres an hour. The fast-swimming modern dolphin has a similar body shape.

39

Dilophosaurus

Dilophosaurus was an unusual dinosaur with two thin crests, shaped like half moons, on its head. It was large and strong but its teeth were thin and it probably did not kill its victims by biting them. Instead, it may have ripped at prey with its clawed hands and feet or fed on the remains of the kills of larger, stronger animals.

SIZE:
6 m long

GROUP:
**Coelurosaur
(carnivorous dinosaur)**

Scelidosaurus

Like all ankylosaurs, *Scelidosaurus* was heavily armoured against attackers. Its back was covered in hard bony plates which were studded with rows of spikes running from neck to tail. It had sturdy legs and probably moved around on all fours, feeding on plants.

SIZE:
4 m long

GROUP:
**Ankylosaur (armoured
dinosaur)**

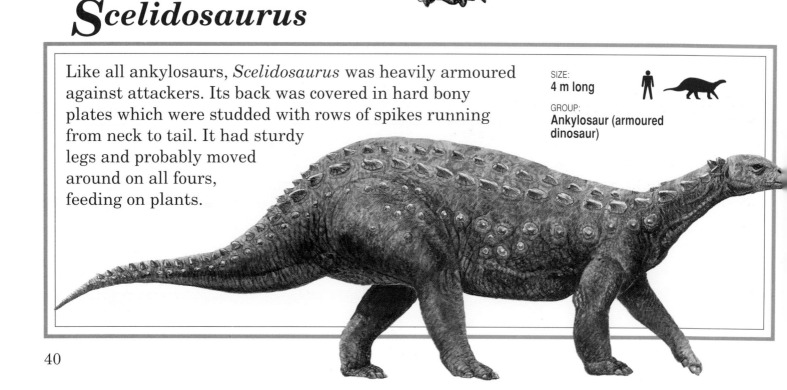

Stenopterygius

Its sleek, torpedo-shaped body, long paddles and fish-like tail helped make *Stenopterygius* a fast, agile swimmer. It fed on fish and squid which it hunted with the aid of its large eyes and sensitive ears. Like other ichthyosaurs, it gave birth to live young in the water.

SIZE:
up to 2 m long

GROUP:
Ichthyosaur (marine reptile)

Protosuchus

This early crocodile was a land-living creature—its remains have been found in the same rocks as many dinosaurs. It could run fast on its long, slim legs, and caught such prey as lizards in its sharp teeth. Like modern crocodiles, *Protosuchus* had a pair of teeth on the lower jaw that fitted into notches on the upper jaw.

SIZE:
1 m long

GROUP:
Crocodylian (crocodile)

Scutellosaurus

Another well-armoured dinosaur, *Scutellosaurus* was covered with rows of bony studs which helped protect it from predators. Its tail was particularly long and was probably held out to help balance the animal when it ran on two legs.

SIZE:
1.2 m long

GROUP:
Ornithopod
(bird-foot dinosaur)

41

Ophthalmosaurus

Pterodactylus

Liopleurodon

Elaphrosaurus

Dicraeosaurus

Life in the Late Jurassic

Most of the Late Jurassic world was much warmer than now, and there was plenty of rain. Plants were generally large and luxuriant, like tropical rain forest plants today.

Forest trees included palm-like cycads, ginkgos—one kind of which still grows today—and many sorts of cone-bearing conifers related to today's pines and firs. Ferns and giant horsetail plants covered the ground around them.

With the mild weather and plenty of plants to feed on, animals flourished, too. The land was still dominated by the dinosaurs, and huge long-necked plant-eaters such as *Diplodocus* wandered the forests. *Compsognathus* and other agile hunters preyed on smaller plant-eating dinosaurs.

Only a few kinds of small shrew-like mammals had evolved. These probably hid in burrows for much of the day and came out at night to search for food.

A European redwood forest

A flying reptile, *Scaphognathus* had long jaws and sharp teeth. It may have fed on insects, which were plentiful in Jurassic forests.

Long-necked *Cetiosauriscus* could reach up and feed on high branches of the forest trees.

Archaeopteryx may have caught insects while in flight or swooped down in surprise attacks on small ground-living creatures.

Palm-like cycads were at their most varied in the Jurassic and grew all over the world. Only a few species survive today.

Ferns were still among the most common plants and covered the forest floor.

Tuojiangosaurus　　　*Yangchuanosaurus*　　　*Brachiosaurus*　　　*Othnielia*　　　*Camptosaurus*

Huge redwood trees, similar to those still growing in North America, once grew in the warm swampy forests of Europe.

The earliest known bird, *Archaeopteryx* could climb trees with the help of the claws on its wings and may have been able to glide or even flap its wings to fly.

Camptosaurus moved on all fours while feeding but could rear up on its back legs to run away from its enemies.

A powerful killer with big curved fangs, *Megalosaurus* preyed on plant-eating dinosaurs.

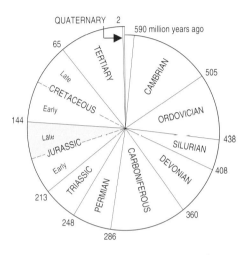

The Jurassic period ended about 144 million years ago.

The map shows the positions of the world's landmasses in the Late Jurassic. At this time, the northern and southern continents were beginning to split away from each other. The land now called North America was at this time separated from the landmass of South America by sea.

The world 170 million years ago

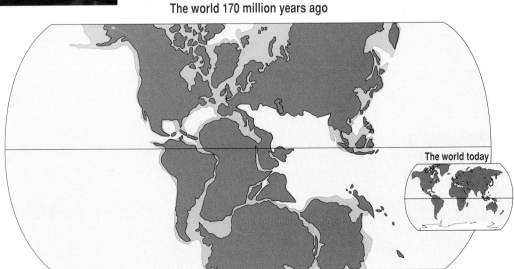

SEA

CONTINENTAL SHELF

LAND

The world today

45

Camptosaurus

Camptosaurus was a relative of the mighty *Iguanodon*. A bulky, heavy creature, it was probably slow-moving and would have spent most of its time on all fours, feeding on low-growing plants. But it could also rear up on its hind legs to reach taller plants and to escape from enemies.

SIZE:
6 m long

GROUP:
Ornithopod
(bird-foot dinosaur)

Scaphognathus

SIZE:
1 m wingspan

GROUP:
Pterosaur
(flying reptile)

Scaphognathus had wings made of skin which it could flap like a modern bird. Its bone structure suggests that it had a poor sense of smell but excellent eyesight, so could probably spot its prey from the air.

Ophthalmosaurus

The super-large eyes of this ichthyosaur suggest that it fed at night. It probably hunted close to the surface of the water, searching for squid. Each eye socket was about 10 centimetres across and a bony ring surrounded each eyeball to prevent it collapsing under the water's pressure.

SIZE:
3.5 m long

GROUP:
Ichthyosaur
(marine reptile)

Liopleurodon

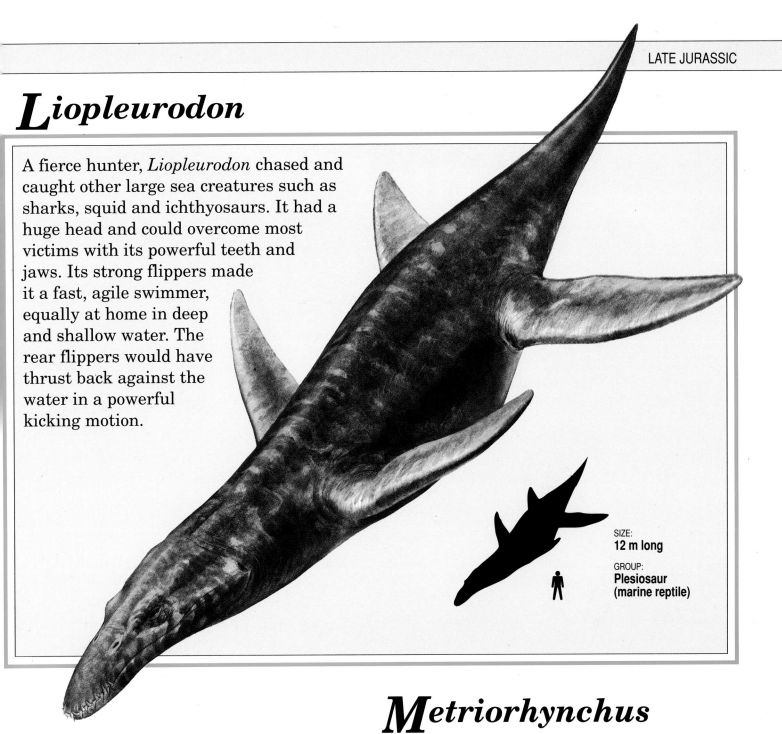

A fierce hunter, *Liopleurodon* chased and caught other large sea creatures such as sharks, squid and ichthyosaurs. It had a huge head and could overcome most victims with its powerful teeth and jaws. Its strong flippers made it a fast, agile swimmer, equally at home in deep and shallow water. The rear flippers would have thrust back against the water in a powerful kicking motion.

SIZE:
12 m long

GROUP:
Plesiosaur (marine reptile)

Metriorhynchus

Metriorhynchus spent its life in the sea. Its legs were paddle-shaped flippers and it had a fin on its tail which powered its swimming. It did not have the body armour of land-living crocodiles—this would have been too heavy in the sea. It fed on fish and squid which it caught in its sharp-toothed jaws.

SIZE:
3 m long

GROUP:
Crocodylian (crocodile)

47

Pterodactylus

There were many different kinds of pterodactyl. Some had wingspans of 60 centimetres, others as large as 12 metres, but most had short tails and long necks. *Pterodactylus* had long narrow jaws, lined with sharp teeth—ideal for catching insects or small fish.

SIZE:
up to 75 cm wingspan

GROUP:
Pterosaur (flying reptile)

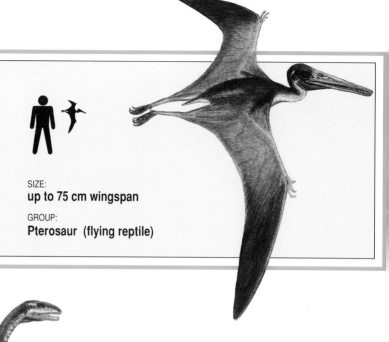

Elaphrosaurus

SIZE:
3.5 m long

GROUP:
Ornithomimid (ostrich dinosaur)

Elaphrosaurus probably belonged to a group known as "ostrich dinosaurs" and did look a lot like a modern ostrich. The only skeleton ever found comes from the famous Tendaguru dinosaur bed in Tanzania, where more than 250 tonnes of dinosaur bones were dug up between 1908 and 1912.

Kentrosaurus

This stegosaur had a double row of narrow bony plates from its neck to the middle of its back. Sharp spikes then completed the line of armour to the end of the tail. More spikes sticking out at hip level on each side gave *Kentrosaurus* extra protection from enemies.

SIZE:
5 m long

GROUP:
Stegosaur (plated dinosaur)

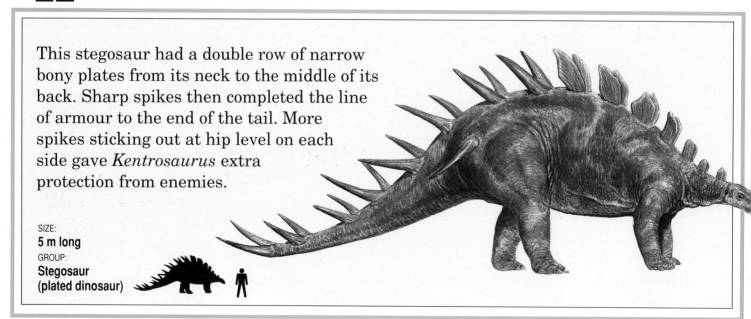

Megalosaurus

Megalosaurus was the first dinosaur ever to be scientifically described and named. It was a massive creature and a fierce hunter. Its head was large and its powerful jaws were armed with curved teeth, serrated like steak knives, for cutting into flesh. On its fingers and toes were sharp claws. With such weapons, *Megalosaurus* could attack the large, plant-eating dinosaurs of the time.

SIZE:
9 m long

GROUP:
Carnosaur (large carnivorous dinosaur)

Dicraeosaurus

A member of the same family as the giant *Diplodocus*, *Dicraeosaurus* was smaller and had a shorter neck. It roamed the tropical plains of eastern Africa, feeding on plants.

SIZE:
12.5 m long

GROUP:
Sauropod (long-necked browsing dinosaur)

Yangchuanosaurus

Huge jaws and fangs like daggers made this dinosaur a fearsome predator. It moved on large pillar-like back legs, holding its tail out stiffly to balance its weight. Both fingers and toes bore sharp claws which helped it seize prey.

SIZE:
up to 10 m long

GROUP:
Carnosaur (large carnivorous dinosaur)

Euhelopus

A plant-eating dinosaur, *Euhelopus* lived in China. It had a long neck and could probably reach up to the lower branches of fir trees and tear away great mouthfuls of the needle-like leaves. Its long, spoon-shaped teeth would have been able to deal with such tough plants.

Tuojiangosaurus

Like all stegosaurs, this creature had rows of bony plates jutting from its back, neck and tail but these plates had more spikes than those of *Stegosaurus*. A slow bulky animal, it would probably have stood its ground if attacked and lashed out with its spiny tail. It fed on plants but had small, weak teeth and could probably only browse on young shoots and ferns.

SIZE:
7 m long

GROUP:
Stegosaur (plated dinosaur)

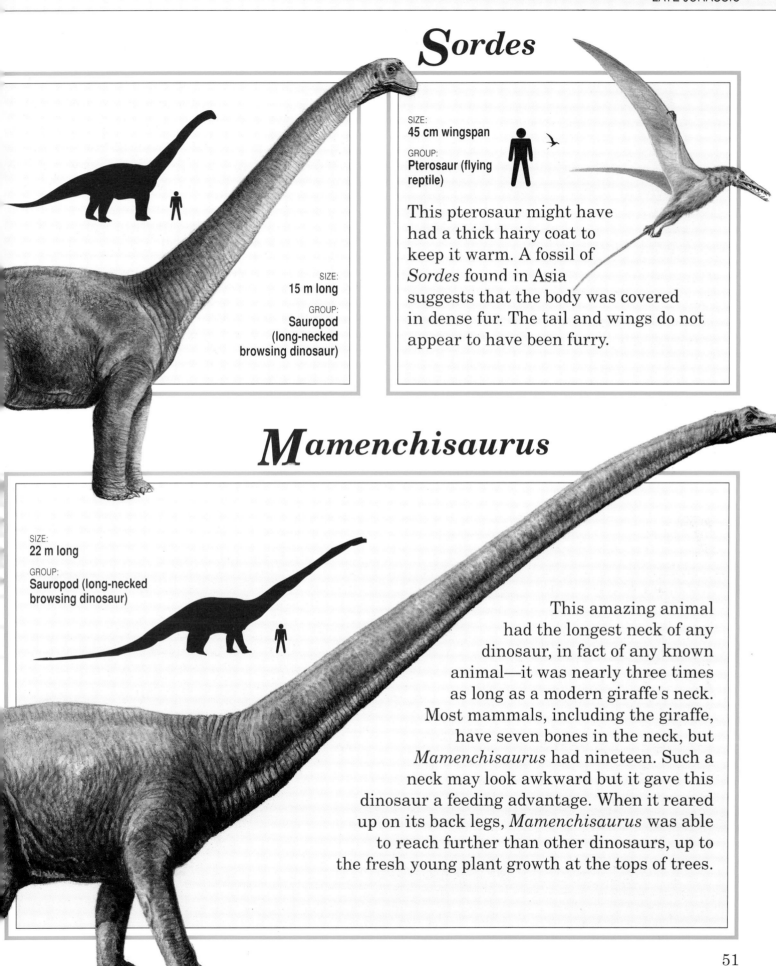

Sordes

SIZE:
45 cm wingspan

GROUP:
Pterosaur (flying reptile)

This pterosaur might have had a thick hairy coat to keep it warm. A fossil of *Sordes* found in Asia suggests that the body was covered in dense fur. The tail and wings do not appear to have been furry.

SIZE:
15 m long

GROUP:
Sauropod (long-necked browsing dinosaur)

Mamenchisaurus

SIZE:
22 m long

GROUP:
Sauropod (long-necked browsing dinosaur)

This amazing animal had the longest neck of any dinosaur, in fact of any known animal—it was nearly three times as long as a modern giraffe's neck. Most mammals, including the giraffe, have seven bones in the neck, but *Mamenchisaurus* had nineteen. Such a neck may look awkward but it gave this dinosaur a feeding advantage. When it reared up on its back legs, *Mamenchisaurus* was able to reach further than other dinosaurs, up to the fresh young plant growth at the tops of trees.

Focus on: STEGOSAURS
the armoured plant-eaters

Stegosaurs first evolved about 170 million years ago, in Jurassic times. There were many different types but the largest was *Stegosaurus,* well known for the broad, bony plates along its back.

Nobody knows quite why *Stegosaurus* had these plates. One possibility is that they made a kind of spiky fence of armour on the back to protect the stegosaur from its enemies.

But many experts now think that the plates had a very different purpose—they may have helped control body temperature. The theory is that the plates were not solid, but honeycomb structures through which large quantities of blood flowed. When turned towards the sun the plates would have absorbed heat and warmed the animal's body. When turned away they would have given off heat and helped the body cool down.

The tail of *Stegosaurus* was lined with pairs of vicious spikes, each about 1 metre long. These spikes were probably covered in horn and were used to help the animal defend itself against predatory dinosaurs. *Stegosaurus* could have swung its heavy, spiked tail from side to side and caused serious damage to an attacker.

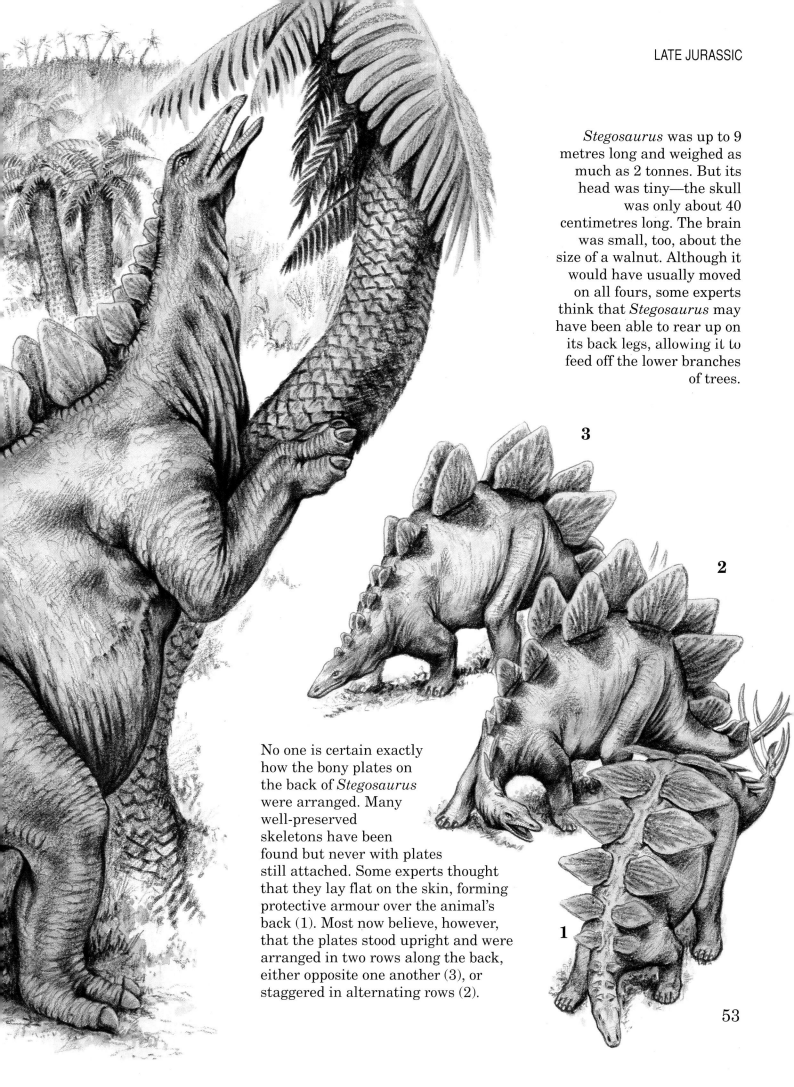

Stegosaurus was up to 9 metres long and weighed as much as 2 tonnes. But its head was tiny—the skull was only about 40 centimetres long. The brain was small, too, about the size of a walnut. Although it would have usually moved on all fours, some experts think that *Stegosaurus* may have been able to rear up on its back legs, allowing it to feed off the lower branches of trees.

3

2

No one is certain exactly how the bony plates on the back of *Stegosaurus* were arranged. Many well-preserved skeletons have been found but never with plates still attached. Some experts thought that they lay flat on the skin, forming protective armour over the animal's back (1). Most now believe, however, that the plates stood upright and were arranged in two rows along the back, either opposite one another (3), or staggered in alternating rows (2).

1

Diplodocus

Diplodocus was one of the longest of all dinosaurs but had light bones in its back and so was not as heavy as other giant plant-eaters. Much of its length was made up of its snaky neck and whip-like tail. Its size alone helped protect it from enemies but *Diplodocus* could also sweep smaller animals away by lashing its mighty tail from side to side. It fed on huge quantities of plants, using its thin, pencil-shaped teeth to strip leaves from branches.

Coelurus

A fast-moving hunter, this slender long-legged dinosaur lived in forests and swamps where prey was plentiful. Its strong hands were armed with three sharp-clawed fingers—ideal for grasping small animals such as lizards and flying reptiles.

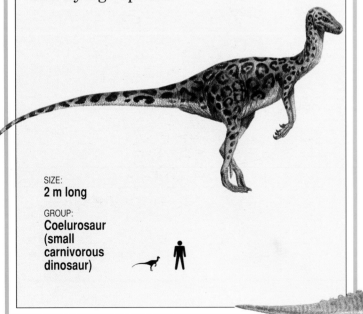

SIZE:
2 m long

GROUP:
Coelurosaur (small carnivorous dinosaur)

Ceratosaurus

Powerful jaws with sharp, curving fangs were this hunter's main weapons. It moved on strong back legs and seized its victims with the clawed fingers on its short arms. On its head *Ceratosaurus* had a small horn, which it may have used in head-butting battles with other males to win leadership of the group.

SIZE:
6 m long

GROUP:
Carnosaur (large carnivorous dinosaur)

SIZE:
26 m long

GROUP:
**Sauropod
(long-necked
browsing dinosaur)**

*A*patosaurus

This massive creature, which would have weighed more than six full-grown elephants, was also called *Brontosaurus,* or "thunder lizard". But scientists found that two different names had been given to the same creature so it is now properly called by the first name given—*Apatosaurus*. It fed on plants and probably had to spend most of its life eating in order to get enough food for its huge body. It had teeth only at the front of its mouth and could not chew, so it just swallowed leaves and other plant material whole.

SIZE:
up to 21 m long

GROUP:
**Sauropod (long-necked
browsing dinosaur)**

Dryosaurus

SIZE:
up to 3 m long

GROUP:
**Ornithopod
(bird-foot dinosaur)**

Dryosaurus was a plant-eating dinosaur that probably lived in herds. Like modern deer, it was a fast runner and, when danger threatened from one of the many fierce hunting dinosaurs, it could sprint away at top speed on its long back legs.

Brachiosaurus

One of the largest, tallest dinosaurs, *Brachiosaurus* stood at least 10 metres high—as big as a four-storey building. It was heavy, too, and weighed an incredible 89 tonnes—about the same as 12 adult elephants. This giant fed on plants which it chewed with the pointed peg-like teeth which lined its jaws. Its front legs were longer than its back legs so, rather like a giraffe, its body sloped down from the shoulders. This helped give its long neck an even greater reach up to leaves on the highest branches.

Allosaurus

The largest and most fearsome predator of its time, *Allosaurus* was a giant killer. Hunting in packs, it probably managed to bring down huge plant-eating dinosaurs such as *Apatosaurus* and *Diplodocus*. *Allosaurus* had a large head and strong neck and its powerful jaws were equipped with more than 70 saw-edged teeth which it used to tear flesh from its victims.

SIZE:
up to 12 m long

GROUP:
Carnosaur (large carnivorous dinosaur)

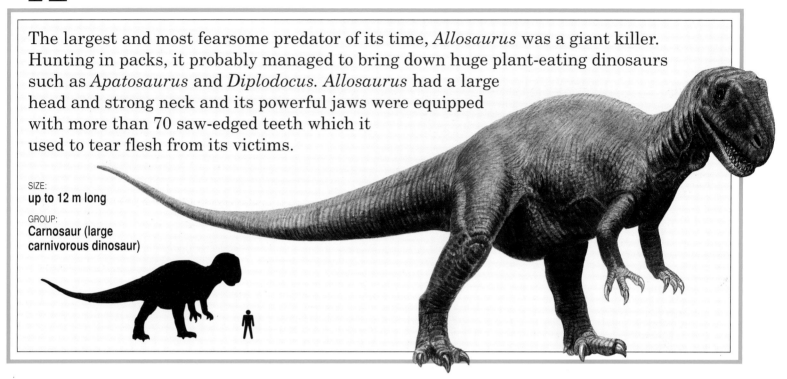

SIZE:
23 m long

GROUP:
Sauropod (long-necked browsing dinosaur)

Othnielia

A small, lightweight creature, *Othnielia* had long legs and tail and short arms with five-fingered hands. It fed on plants which it plucked with the hard toothless beak at the front of its jaws, and then ground down with the strong teeth further back in its mouth.

SIZE:
1.5 m long

GROUP:
Ornithopod (bird-foot dinosaur)

57

Dsungaripterus   *Bernissartia*   *Iguanodon*   *Psittacosaurus*   *Hypsilophodon*

Life in the Early Cretaceous

By the Early Cretaceous the single huge continent of Triassic times had split into northern and southern landmasses. These supercontinents were breaking up into smaller areas of land—Africa, for example, had started to drift away from South America.

The beginning of the Cretaceous period was also the beginning of the modern world of plants. Non-flowering plants such as ferns, horsetails, conifers and cycads still dominated the land, but the very first of the flowering plants that would eventually cover much of the land surface of the planet, were evolving.

Flowering plants may have first appeared in tropical South America and Africa. Their light seeds were easily carried by the wind and they would have quickly spread around the world.

Plant-eating dinosaurs took full advantage of this new food supply and thrived. There was a greater range of dinosaurs than ever before.

An Asian river delta

Iguanodon mongolensis had strong teeth and powerful beak-like jaws. It browsed on tough, low-growing plants such as horsetails.

Cycadeoids seemed to have had structures which looked almost like flowers, covered with hairy scales.

Cycads were cone-bearing plants. There were male and female plants, each with different cones.

Conifer trees were among the largest plants in the Early Cretaceous.

Dsungaripterus was a pterodactyl—a flying reptile with a wingspan of about 3 metres.

Deinonychus   Echinodon   Hylaeosaurus   Acrocanthosaurus   Baryonyx

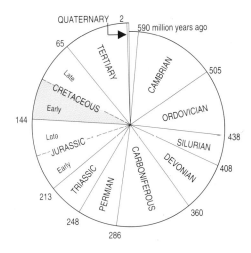

Wuerhosaurus was a stegosaur or plated dinosaur. It fed on plants.

Euhelopus probably lived in both the Late Jurassic and Early Cretaceous. With the help of its long neck it could reach high into the trees for food.

The Cretaceous period began about 144 million years ago. Its name comes from a Latin word meaning "of chalk" and refers to the many chalk deposits made in the shallow seas that covered much of Europe and North America later in the period.

The map shows how the world might have looked in the Early Cretaceous period as the northern and southern landmasses split further apart.

Horsetails were moisture-loving plants that grew near lakes and streams.

A relative of *Iguanodon*, *Probactrosaurus* was a plant-eating dinosaur.

The world 140 million years ago

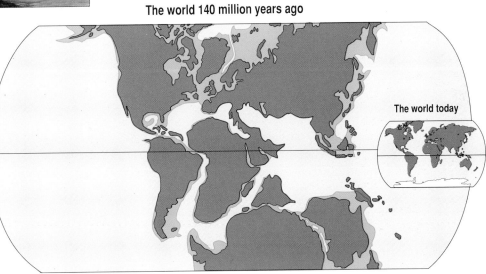

- ☐ SEA
- ☐ CONTINENTAL SHELF
- ☐ LAND

The world today

61

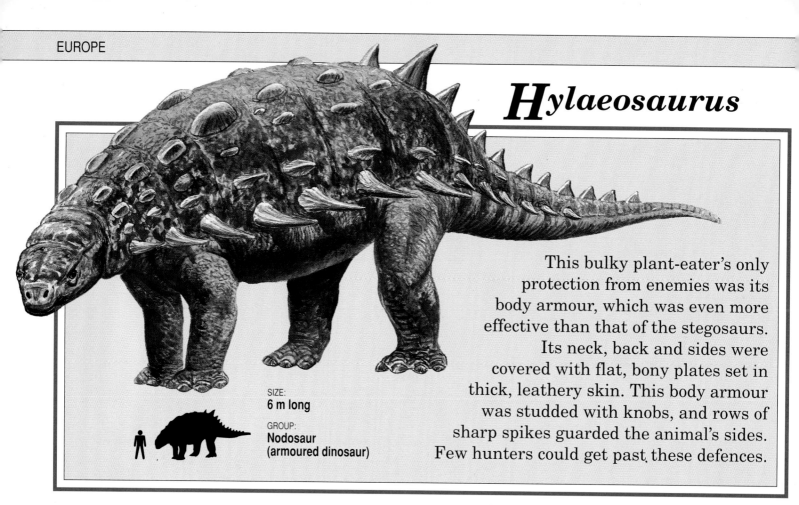

Hylaeosaurus

SIZE:
6 m long

GROUP:
**Nodosaur
(armoured dinosaur)**

This bulky plant-eater's only protection from enemies was its body armour, which was even more effective than that of the stegosaurs. Its neck, back and sides were covered with flat, bony plates set in thick, leathery skin. This body armour was studded with knobs, and rows of sharp spikes guarded the animal's sides. Few hunters could get past these defences.

Echinodon

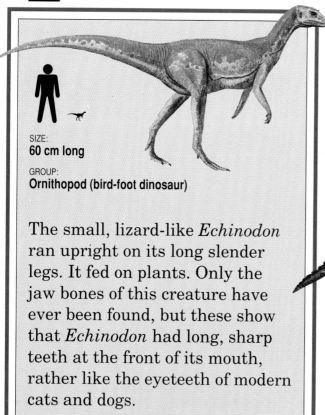

SIZE:
60 cm long

GROUP:
Ornithopod (bird-foot dinosaur)

The small, lizard-like *Echinodon* ran upright on its long slender legs. It fed on plants. Only the jaw bones of this creature have ever been found, but these show that *Echinodon* had long, sharp teeth at the front of its mouth, rather like the eyeteeth of modern cats and dogs.

Bernissartia

This tiny crocodile probably lived on land and in the water, judging by the two types of teeth in its jaws. At the front were long, pointed teeth, suitable for catching fish. Further back in its mouth were broad, flat teeth for crushing shellfish or even the bones of dead animals.

SIZE:
60 cm long

GROUP:
Crocodylian (crocodile)

62

Baryonyx

Baryonyx was only discovered in 1983, so experts are still figuring out how it lived from the clues given by its skeleton. It had a long, narrow head like a crocodile's, and jaws with twice as many teeth as most carnosaurs—this may mean it was a fish-eater. It also had a curved claw, about 30 centimetres long, on each of its front feet. This would have made an excellent weapon and may even have been used to hook fish out of the water.

SIZE:
6 m long

GROUP:
Carnosaur (large carnivorous dinosaur)

Iguanodon

SIZE:
9 m long

GROUP:
Ornithopod (bird-foot dinosaur)

A plant-eater, this mighty creature lived in herds, roaming the lush Cretaceous landscape in search of ferns and horsetails. *Iguanodon*'s hands were unusual. They were well suited both for walking on and for grasping food, and on each there was a sharp spike that made a useful weapon.

Dsungaripterus

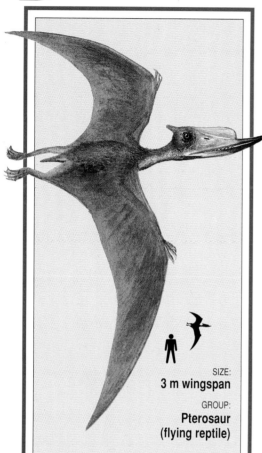

SIZE:
3 m wingspan

GROUP:
**Pterosaur
(flying reptile)**

Dsungaripterus had an
unusual bony crest
along its snout and
long, narrow jaws that
curved upwards to a
fine point at the tip.
These jaws looked a
little like forceps but
were paper-thin. How
these jaws were used
is still not known. Like
all other pterosaurs,
Dsungaripterus flew
on large leathery wings
made of skin.

SIZE:
6 m long

GROUP:
**Stegosaur
(plated dinosaur)**

Probactrosaurus

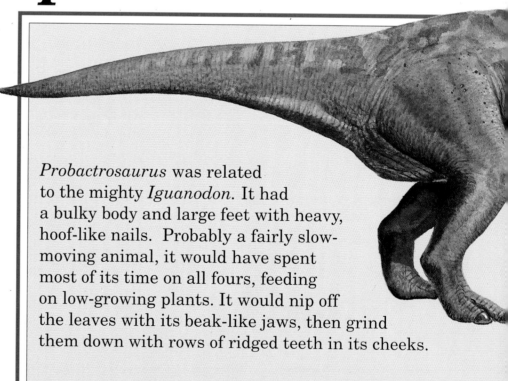

Probactrosaurus was related
to the mighty *Iguanodon*. It had
a bulky body and large feet with heavy,
hoof-like nails. Probably a fairly slow-
moving animal, it would have spent
most of its time on all fours, feeding
on low-growing plants. It would nip off
the leaves with its beak-like jaws, then grind
them down with rows of ridged teeth in its cheeks.

Wuerhosaurus

Only a few bones of this stegosaur have ever been found, so its reconstruction is partly guesswork. Like all stegosaurs, it seems to have had a series of triangular-shaped plates along its back and sharp spines on its tail. *Wuerhosaurus* was a plant-eater and moved around on four legs.

Pachyrhachis

This creature had a long, slender body like a snake, but a head more like a lizard. It lived in water and probably swam by wriggling movements of its supple body.

SIZE:
1 m long

GROUP:
**Serpentes
(aquatic reptile)**

Psittacosaurus

SIZE:
up to 2.5 m long

GROUP:
**Ceratopian
(horned dinosaur)**

This strange creature had a large head armed with a horny parrot-like beak—its name means "parrot lizard". It had no teeth but its beak was sharp and could slice through tough leaves and stems.

SIZE:
6 m long

GROUP:
**Ornithopod
(bird-foot dinosaur)**

Focus on: PTEROSAURS
the flying reptiles

Pterosaurs were among the first vertebrates—animals with backbones—to take to life in the air. These flying reptiles flew on wings made of skin, attached to the extra long fourth fingers of each hand.

Pterosaurs first evolved in Late Triassic times, 50 million years before the first known bird, *Archaeopteryx,* appeared. They flourished all through the Jurassic period and finally became extinct at the same time as the dinosaurs, about 65 million years ago.

There were two sorts of pterosaurs. First came the rhamphorhynchoids, such as *Rhamphorhynchus* and *Anurognathus,* which had short legs and long, bony tails. Later came the pterodactyloids, such as *Pterodaustro* and *Quetzalcoatlus*, which were similar but had shorter tails and longer necks.

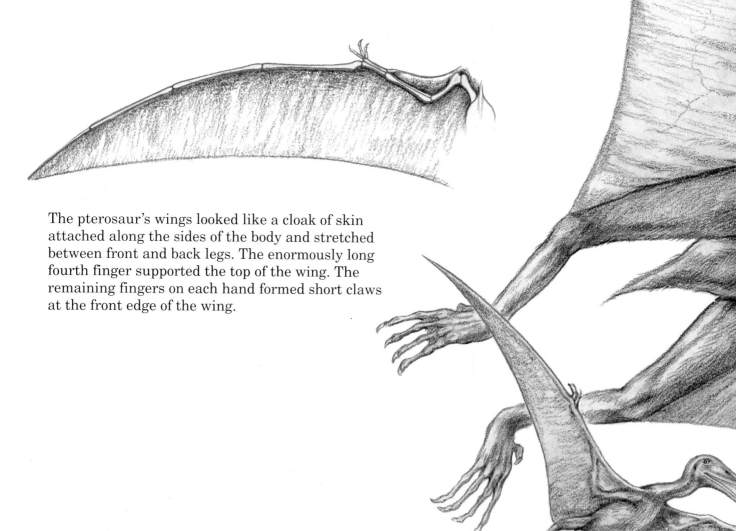

The pterosaur's wings looked like a cloak of skin attached along the sides of the body and stretched between front and back legs. The enormously long fourth finger supported the top of the wing. The remaining fingers on each hand formed short claws at the front edge of the wing.

Pterodaustro

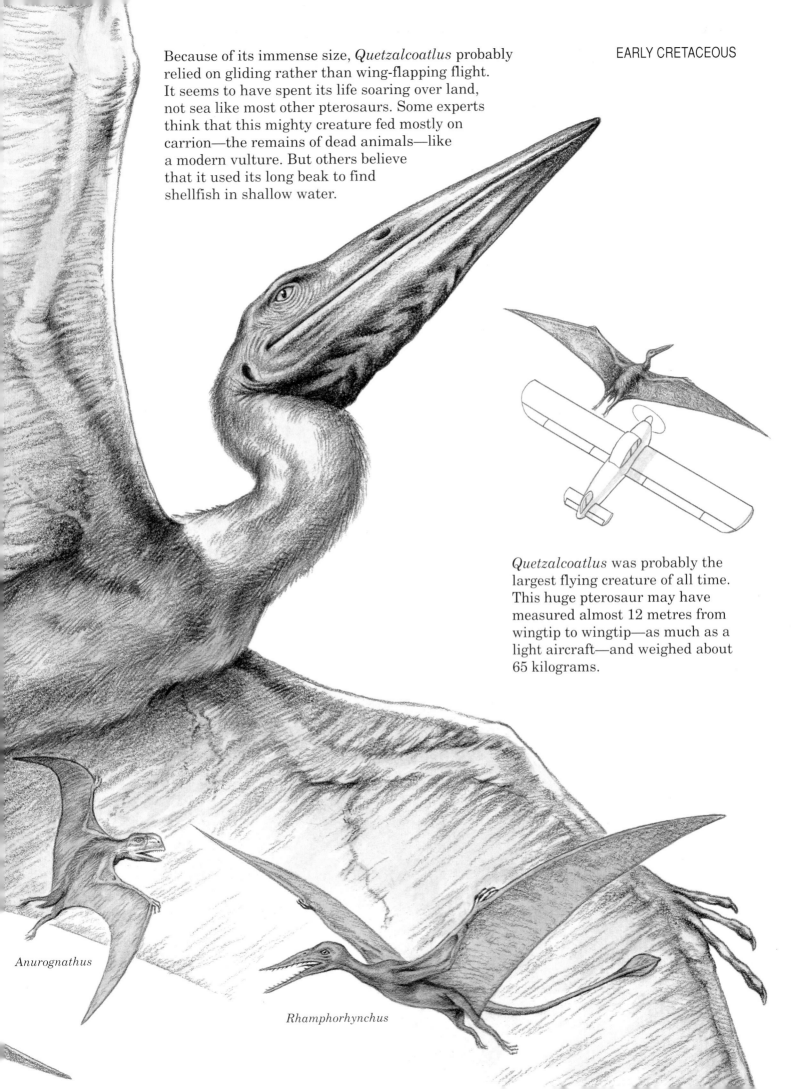

Because of its immense size, *Quetzalcoatlus* probably relied on gliding rather than wing-flapping flight. It seems to have spent its life soaring over land, not sea like most other pterosaurs. Some experts think that this mighty creature fed mostly on carrion—the remains of dead animals—like a modern vulture. But others believe that it used its long beak to find shellfish in shallow water.

Quetzalcoatlus was probably the largest flying creature of all time. This huge pterosaur may have measured almost 12 metres from wingtip to wingtip—as much as a light aircraft—and weighed about 65 kilograms.

Anurognathus

Rhamphorhynchus

Acrocanthosaurus

A powerfully built hunter, *Acrocanthosaurus* killed and ate other dinosaurs. The name of this large creature means "top-spined lizard". This refers to the ridge of skin, held up by spines rising from the backbone, running from neck to tail.

SIZE:
13 m long

GROUP:
Carnosaur (large carnivorous dinosaur)

Sauropelta

This peaceful plant-eater could not run fast, but its armour protected it from hunting carnivorous dinosaurs. It had bands of strong bony plates across its back and rows of sharp spikes on each side.

SIZE:
7.5 m long

GROUP:
Ankylosaur (armoured dinosaur)

SIZE:
3-4 m long

GROUP:
Deinonychosaur (terrible-clawed dinosaur)

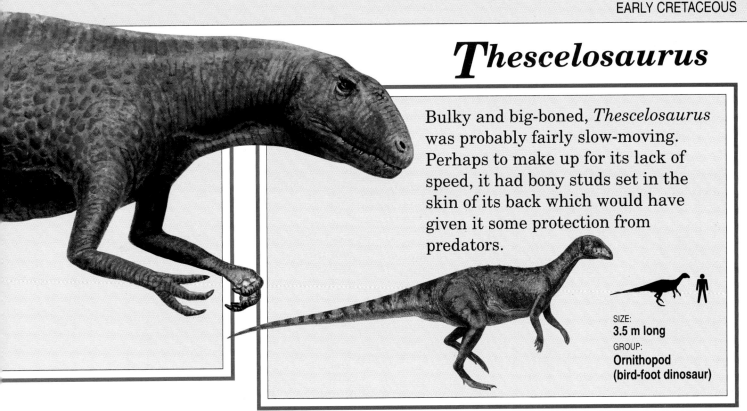

Thescelosaurus

Bulky and big-boned, *Thescelosaurus* was probably fairly slow-moving. Perhaps to make up for its lack of speed, it had bony studs set in the skin of its back which would have given it some protection from predators.

SIZE:
3.5 m long
GROUP:
**Ornithopod
(bird-foot dinosaur)**

Deinonychus

Tenontosaurus

Fast-moving *Deinonychus* or "terrible claw" was built for killing. It had a large head, equipped with jagged teeth for tearing at lumps of flesh. On each foot was a huge curved, 12-centimetre claw. Standing on one leg it could slash at its victims.

A large, bulky dinosaur with a long, extremely thick tail, *Tenontosaurus* was a plant-eater. Although it could kick with its clawed feet and use its heavy tail as a whiplash, it would have been no match for fierce fast-moving hunters such as *Deinonychus*.

SIZE:
7.5 m long
GROUP:
Ornithopod (bird-foot dinosaur)

69

Life in the Late Cretaceous

Flowering plants, which first appeared in the Early Cretaceous, were beginning to dominate the land by the Late Cretaceous. Hickory trees, oaks and magnolias were all flourishing in addition to smaller flowering plants. The variety of plants provided a great range of food for the plant-eaters.

There was also a greater variety of dinosaurs then than at any other time. But at the end of the Cretaceous, about 65 million years ago, they all became extinct.

No one is really sure why they disappeared. One popular theory is that a huge meteorite hit the Earth, throwing vast amounts of dust into the air. The dust in the atmosphere would have blocked the sun's light and killed off many land plants. This could have caused the death of plant-eating dinosaurs and, in turn, of the flesh-eating dinosaurs that fed on them.

The birds of today are the only living descendants of the dinosaurs.

72

A North American forest

Pteranodon was one of the longest winged of all pterosaurs. It soared high above the land on rising hot air currents.

Parasaurolophus had a single tube-like crest on its head. This crest was hollow and may have helped make the animal's honking calls louder.

Cycadeoids were cycad-like plants with cones, which became extinct toward the end of the Cretaceous.

Flowering plants such as magnolias were starting to fill the forests of North America at this time.

Alphadon was an early marsupial—a pouched mammal. It could climb well and probably spent much of its life in trees.

Stegoceras

Triceratops

Alamosaurus

Torosaurus

Ankylosaurus

In this North American forest, storm clouds darken the sky as a *Tyrannosaurus* thunders into view and the peaceful plant-eaters scatter in alarm.

A young *Corythosaurus* had a much smaller head crest than the adult. The crest gradually developed as the animal grew.

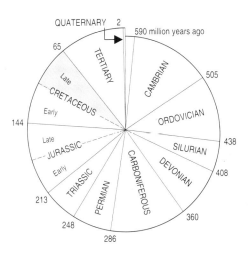

The Late Cretaceous ended about 65 million years ago and with it ended the age of the dinosaurs.

The map shows the positions of the world's landmasses in the Late Cretaceous period. At this time shallow seas had invaded North America and Europe, dividing the land in the northern half of the world.

The mighty *Tyrannosaurus* was heavier than an elephant. It was the top predator in Cretaceous forests.

Corythosaurus lived in herds, wandering the forests in search of food such as pine needles and magnolia leaves.

The world 100 million years ago

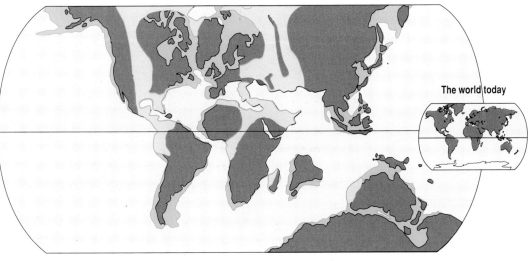

The world today

☐ SEA

▨ CONTINENTAL SHELF

▨ LAND

☐ SHALLOW SEA

73

*P*latecarpus

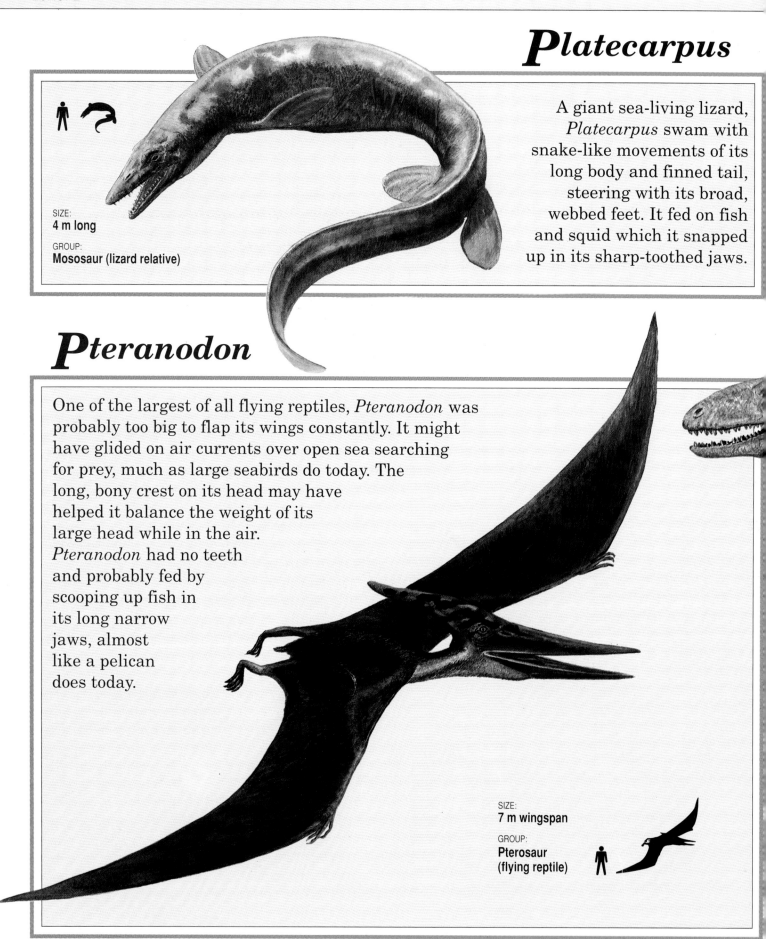

SIZE:
4 m long

GROUP:
Mososaur (lizard relative)

A giant sea-living lizard, *Platecarpus* swam with snake-like movements of its long body and finned tail, steering with its broad, webbed feet. It fed on fish and squid which it snapped up in its sharp-toothed jaws.

*P*teranodon

One of the largest of all flying reptiles, *Pteranodon* was probably too big to flap its wings constantly. It might have glided on air currents over open sea searching for prey, much as large seabirds do today. The long, bony crest on its head may have helped it balance the weight of its large head while in the air. *Pteranodon* had no teeth and probably fed by scooping up fish in its long narrow jaws, almost like a pelican does today.

SIZE:
7 m wingspan

GROUP:
**Pterosaur
(flying reptile)**

Struthiosaurus

Struthiosaurus was smaller than most armoured dinosaurs but was protected by several different sorts of body armour. There were tough plates around its neck, small bony studs covered the back and tail, and a fringe of spikes guarded each flank.

SIZE:
2 m long

GROUP:
**Nodosaur
(armoured dinosaur)**

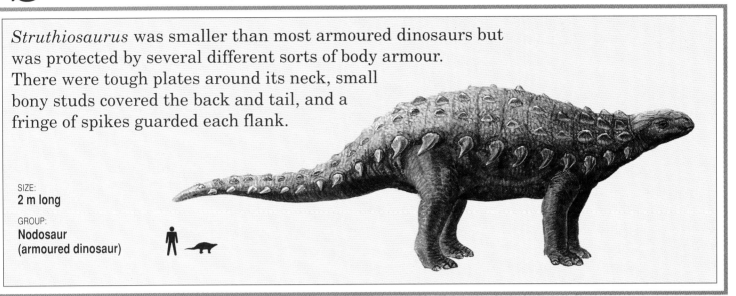

Eustreptospondylus

SIZE:
7 m long

GROUP:
**Carnosaur
(large carnivorous dinosaur)**

This powerful hunter could walk upright, leaving its short, strong arms free for holding prey. Its head was large and the long jaws were equipped with many saw-edged teeth, ideal for tearing flesh. The long back legs could support its great body weight, yet were light enough to allow the creature to chase swiftly after prey.

Tarbosaurus

This giant, with its huge head and jaws and terrifying fangs, lumbered around eating anything it came across, whether dead or alive. It could have preyed on plant-eating duckbilled and armoured dinosaurs, but, because it was so big, *Tarbosaurus* probably could not move very fast, and may have also fed on the kills of other animals. It was powerful enough to scare off most other predators.

SIZE:
up to 14 m long

GROUP:
Carnosaur (large carnivorous dinosaur)

Protoceratops

A bulky, four-legged plant-eater, *Protoceratops* had a strong beak, shaped like a parrot's, and a large frill, made of a sheet of bone, at the back of its neck. The first dinosaur eggs and nests ever found belonged to this dinosaur. And inside some of these nests, dug about 80 million years ago, tiny fossilized bones of baby *Protoceratops* have been found.

SIZE:
3 m long

GROUP:
Ceratopian (horned dinosaur)

Velociraptor

This ferocious two-legged killer grasped its victims with its strong arms while attacking them with the large claws on each foot. Fossilized skeletons have been found of *Velociraptor* locked in battle with a horned dinosaur.

SIZE:
2 m long

GROUP:
**Deinonychosaur
(terrible-clawed dinosaur)**

Alioramus

Like its larger relative, *Tyrannosaurus*, *Alioramus* was a fierce hunter, with a large, strong body and heavily clawed feet. On its head were some bony knobs or spikes. These knobs may have been larger on the male *Alioramus* and used in displays for attracting a mate.

SIZE:
6 m long

GROUP:
**Carnosaur
(large carnivorous
dinosaur)**

Elasmosaurus

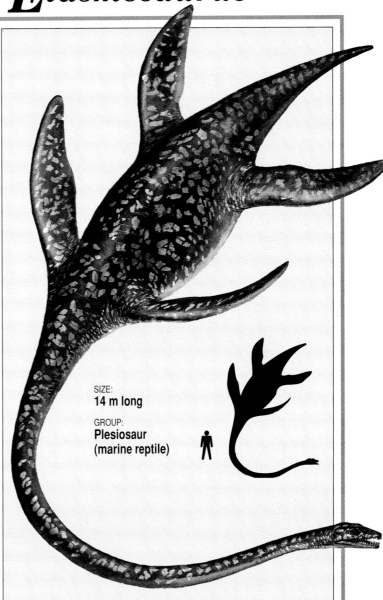

SIZE:
14 m long

GROUP:
**Plesiosaur
(marine reptile)**

The longest known plesiosaur, *Elasmosaurus* had a snake-like neck which was more than half its total body length. The reptile lived in the sea and probably paddled along near the surface, its neck held clear of the water. When it spotted a fish or other creature, *Elasmosaurus* may have plunged its long neck into the sea and snapped up the prey.

*T*sintaosaurus

Until recently, scientists believed that this plant-eating dinosaur had a horn, like that of a unicorn, pointing straight up from between its eyes. The latest evidence, however, suggests that this horn may have pointed backwards, or even that *Tsintaosaurus* did not have a horn at all.

SIZE:
10 m long

GROUP:
**Ornithopod
(bird-foot dinosaur)**

SIZE:
about 12 m long

GROUP:
**Sauropod (long-necked
browsing dinosaur)**

SIZE:
13 m long

GROUP:
**Ornithopod
(bird-foot dinosaur)**

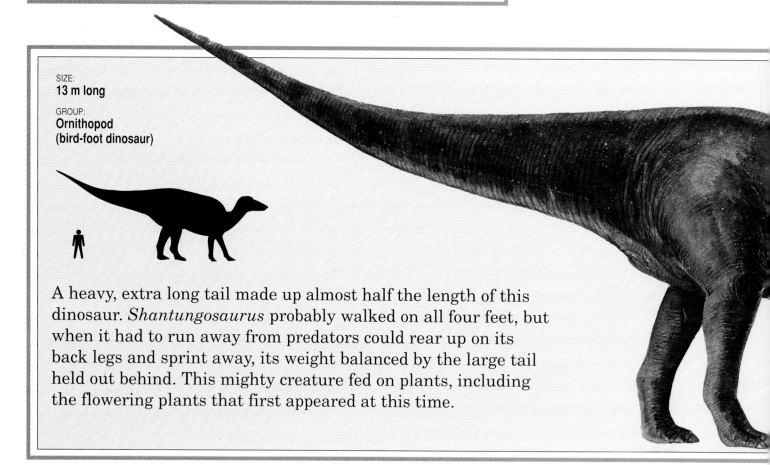

A heavy, extra long tail made up almost half the length of this dinosaur. *Shantungosaurus* probably walked on all four feet, but when it had to run away from predators could rear up on its back legs and sprint away, its weight balanced by the large tail held out behind. This mighty creature fed on plants, including the flowering plants that first appeared at this time.

Opisthocoelicaudia

The one skeleton of this dinosaur found so far lacks its neck and head, so its exact size can only be guessed at. The rest of the body showed that it was a large plant-eating animal, with a long, strong tail. It probably used this tail as a prop, a "third leg", to steady itself when it reared up on its back legs to feed on the leaves of tall trees.

Shantungosaurus

Saichania

A strongly armoured, plant-eating dinosaur, *Saichania* had a massive head studded with bony knobs. Spines stuck out from each side of its body and the whole of its back was protected by rows of knobby plates. Its tail ended in a bony club which could be swung from side to side to fend off attackers.

SIZE:
7 m long

GROUP:
Ankylosaur (armoured dinosaur)

79

Focus on: TYRANNOSAURS
the tyrant lizards

The largest meat-eating animals that have ever lived belonged to the tyrannosaur family—the name means "tyrant lizards". These huge creatures were alive in the Late Cretaceous period, about 80 million years ago, and their remains have been found in Asia and western North America.

Like all the tyrant lizards, *Tyrannosaurus* had a big head and short body, balanced by a long tail. Pillar-like legs with large clawed feet supported its weight. Its arms were puny compared to the rest of the body and were so short they could not even have reached up to the animal's mouth. There were only two fingers on each hand.

Tyrannosaurus probably preyed on the plant-eating dinosaurs roaming North America, such as *Anatosaurus*. Although these creatures were also large, they were no match for powerful tyrannosaurs.

Vicious claws, a strong head and neck, and powerful jaws would have made *Tyrannosaurus* an efficient killer. It probably relied on the surprise attack, charging its victim in a short burst of speed.

Tyrannosaurus looks every bit the fearsome hunter, but some experts have suggested that it might have been a scavenger that fed on kills made by other animals. It could have used its terrifying bulk to frighten other hunters away from their meals.

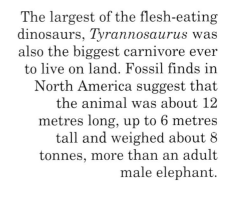

The largest of the flesh-eating dinosaurs, *Tyrannosaurus* was also the biggest carnivore ever to live on land. Fossil finds in North America suggest that the animal was about 12 metres long, up to 6 metres tall and weighed about 8 tonnes, more than an adult male elephant.

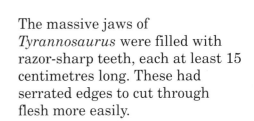

The massive jaws of *Tyrannosaurus* were filled with razor-sharp teeth, each at least 15 centimetres long. These had serrated edges to cut through flesh more easily.

81

Struthiomimus

With its long legs and neck, small head and beak-like mouth, *Struthiomimus* looked very much like an ostrich. All it lacked was feathers. It probably ate a wide variety of food, including leaves, fruit, insects and small animals. When in danger it could run away at high speed—up to 50 kilometres an hour.

Deinosuchus

At three times the size of the biggest crocodiles today, *Deinosuchus* deserved its name, which means "terrible crocodile". It lived in the swamps and probably preyed on dinosaurs by lying in wait and grabbing them as they passed.

SIZE:
possibly 15 m long

GROUP:
Crocodylian (crocodile)

Daspletosaurus

SIZE:
8.5 m long

GROUP:
Carnosaur (large carnivorous dinosaur)

Huge jaws armed with dagger-like fangs, clawed feet and sheer bulk—these were the weapons of this two-legged predator. It probably lay in wait for the large, horned dinosaurs that roamed the forests, and then pounced on its prey with all the force of its 4-tonne body.

Saurolophus

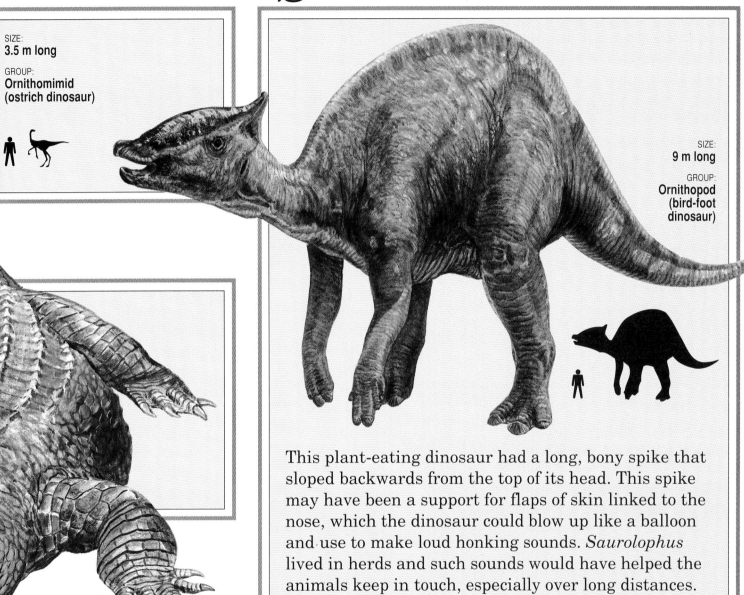

This plant-eating dinosaur had a long, bony spike that sloped backwards from the top of its head. This spike may have been a support for flaps of skin linked to the nose, which the dinosaur could blow up like a balloon and use to make loud honking sounds. *Saurolophus* lived in herds and such sounds would have helped the animals keep in touch, especially over long distances.

Champsosaurus

Champsosaurus lived in rivers and swamps in Europe as well as North America. It was not a crocodile but swam like one, moving its long body and tail from side to side and keeping its legs tucked against its sides. It fed mainly on fish which it caught in its long narrow jaws.

Stegoceras

SIZE:
2 m long

GROUP:
**Pachycephalosaur
(thick-headed dinosaur)**

Stegoceras had a high, domed head, made up of enormously thickened bones. It probably lived in herds and males would have fought for leadership. In these duels the animals charged with heads lowered so that their ramming, domed surfaces met when they crashed together.

Stenonychosaurus

The "brainiest" of them all, *Stenonychosaurus* had the largest brain for its body size of any dinosaur. Its eyes, too, were big—some 5 centimetres across. Such eyes would have made it a good night-time hunter and it was probably active after dark, running through the woods to hunt down small mammals and reptiles.

SIZE:
2 m long

GROUP:
**Coelurosaur (small
carnivorous dinosaur)**

Prosaurolophus

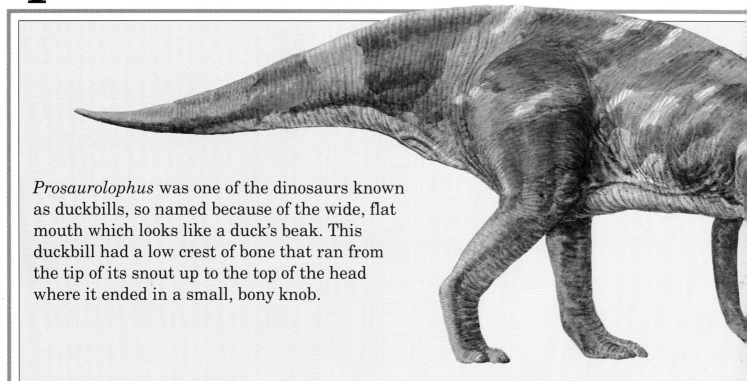

Prosaurolophus was one of the dinosaurs known as duckbills, so named because of the wide, flat mouth which looks like a duck's beak. This duckbill had a low crest of bone that ran from the tip of its snout up to the top of the head where it ended in a small, bony knob.

Plotosaurus

This giant lizard lived in the sea, probably in shallow coastal waters. It had a long tail ending in a fin which must have helped move its great body through the water. Its limbs had developed into flippers, the front pair longer than the back. *Plotosaurus* would have eaten fish, squid and maybe shellfish, snapping them all up in its long, sharp-toothed jaws.

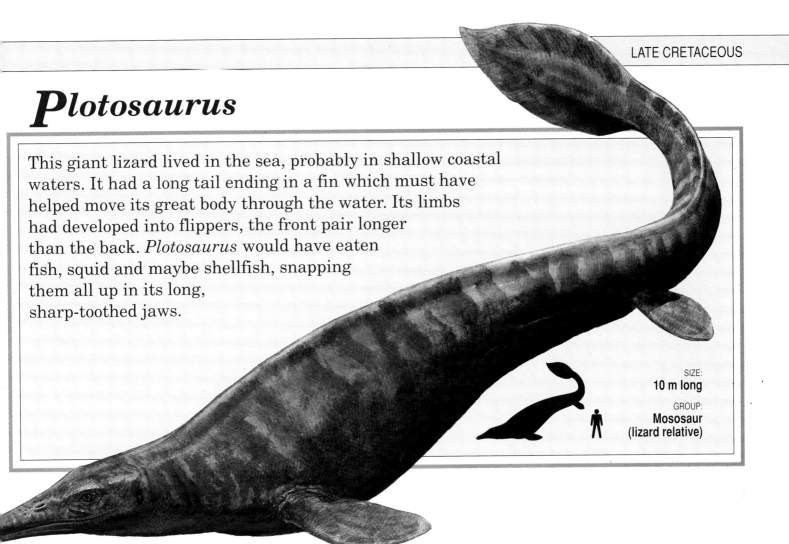

SIZE:
10 m long

GROUP:
Mososaur
(lizard relative)

Parksosaurus

This small, plant-eating dinosaur lived in herds. A fast runner, *Parksosaurus* could run off at high speed if danger threatened. It probably found most of its food on the ground, snuffling about in the undergrowth and nipping off leaves in its narrow, beaked jaws.

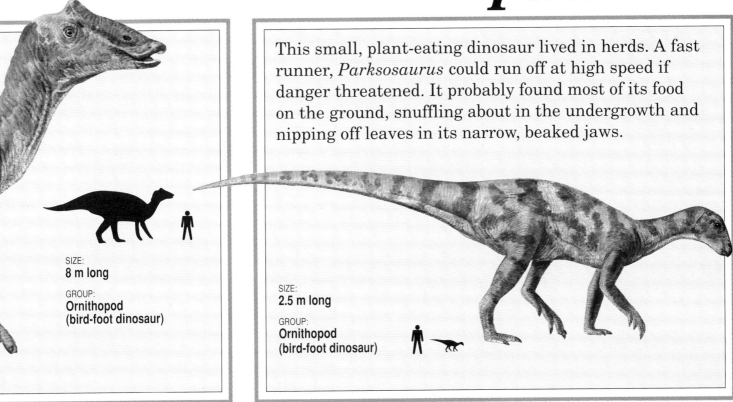

SIZE:
8 m long

GROUP:
Ornithopod
(bird-foot dinosaur)

SIZE:
2.5 m long

GROUP:
Ornithopod
(bird-foot dinosaur)

85

Panoplosaurus

Encased in heavy body armour, *Panoplosaurus* could have weighed as much as an elephant. Square plates and bony studs covered its neck and back, and massive spikes guarded each side. Even its head was protected by bony plates. A plant-eater, it had a narrow snout and may have searched around on the ground for its food.

SIZE:
4.5 m long

GROUP:
Nodosaur
(armoured dinosaur)

Pachycephalosaurus

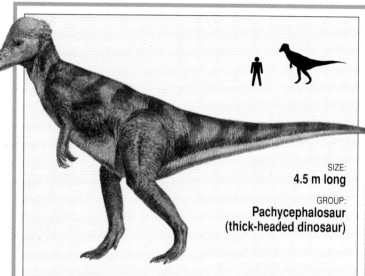

SIZE:
4.5 m long

GROUP:
Pachycephalosaur
(thick-headed dinosaur)

The huge dome on the head of this plant-eater was made of solid bone, 25 centimetres thick. Like a giant crash helmet, this dome absorbed the impact when *Pachycephalosaurus* had head-butting battles with rival males.

Corythosaurus

SIZE:
9 m long

GROUP:
Ornithopod
(bird-foot
dinosaur)

Corythosaurus wandered the forests, feeding on tough pine needles as well as the leaves, seeds and fruits of flowering plants which had evolved by then. A magnificent crest, shaped like a half moon, decorated its head. This crest was hollow and may have helped the animal make loud calls as messages between members of the herd. If danger threatened, these fast runners could dash away on two legs.

*P*arasaurolophus

This dinosaur had a long, thin crest topping its head, which fitted neatly into a notch in its backbone. It may have held the crest in this position when running through dense forest so that the crest swept low-hanging branches upwards, away from the body.

SIZE:
10 m long

GROUP:
**Ornithopod
(bird-foot dinosaur)**

*A*lamosaurus

By the end of the Late Cretaceous period, 65 million years ago, much of North America had turned into wet swampy jungle. But there were still some high, dry places in the southwest where *Alamosaurus* and other sauropods lived, feeding on plants. *Alamosaurus* is named after the Alamo, the famous fortress in Texas.

SIZE:
21 m long

GROUP:
Sauropod (long-necked browsing dinosaur)

Focus on: MAIASAURA
the "good mother lizard"

Like all reptiles, including the turtles alive today, dinosaurs laid eggs with tough waterproof shells inside which the baby could develop in safety.

Turtles lay their eggs in a pit in the ground, then leave them to take their chances. It was long thought that dinosaurs did the same, but recent finds in North America show that many dinosaurs guarded and cared for their young.

Groups of nests were discovered; near them were the skeletons of adult, young and baby dinosaurs. This suggests that the adults stayed near their eggs and probably brought food to the young dinosaurs. The most interesting group of dinosaur nests found belonged to *Maiasaura*, whose name means "good mother lizard".

Clusters of nests in the same area suggest that *Maiasaura* nested in groups. Each nest was made of a mound of earth and sand. The dinosaur scraped out a hollow in the middle to make a safe pit for the eggs.

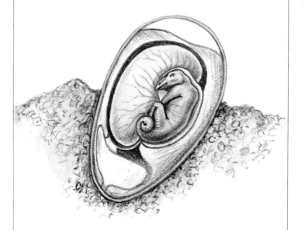

Each egg was about 20 centimetres long—roughly three times the size of a chicken's egg. *Maiasaura* probably laid 20 or more eggs at a time and covered them with sand or plants to help keep them warm and safe.

Maiasaura would have been too heavy to actually sit on her eggs. But she probably kept close guard.

88

Maiasaura was a duckbilled dinosaur, or hadrosaur, that lived in North America in the Late Cretaceous period. It was about 6 metres long and fed on plants. The discovery of a *Maiasaura* nest site in Montana in 1978 has given a new insight into dinosaur family life. The nests were up to 7 metres apart, just room for the mother to lie beside her eggs.

By the time the baby dinosaurs struggled out of their eggs they were about 35 centimetres long. Their mother probably brought them food until they grew strong enough to go and find their own. Since *Maiasaura* nested in groups, there would always have been some adults around to guard the young while others were off gathering leaves and other food.

89

*A**natosaurus*

Two mummified bodies
of this dinosaur have been
found with even the
contents of their
stomachs preserved,
a very rare discovery.
The last meal of these
plant-eaters was pine
needles, twigs, seeds and
fruits. *Anatosaurus* was a duckbilled dinosaur—it
had a horny toothless beak which looked like a duck's bill.

*P**achyrhinosaurus*

SIZE:
5 m long

GROUP:
**Ceratopian
(horned dinosaur)**

Instead of horns, this dinosaur had a
large thick pad of bone above the eyes.
Scientists believe that this pad might
have been used in head-butting fights
with rival males.

*N**odosaurus*

Hundreds of broad, bony plates studded
with little, bony bumps protected this
dinosaur's body—its name means
"lumpy lizard". Its shoulders and legs
were extra strong to carry the weight
of all this armour.

SIZE:
5 m long

GROUP:
**Nodosaur
(armoured dinosaur)**

90

Archelon

This gigantic turtle, more than twice the size of the largest modern turtles, did not have a heavy plated shell. On its back was a bony framework, probably covered by a thick coat of tough, leathery skin. Its beak was toothless and its jaws weak so it may have fed mainly on the soft bodies of jellyfish.

SIZE:
3.5 m long

GROUP:
Chelonian (turtle)

SIZE:
10 m long

GROUP:
**Ornithopod
(bird-foot dinosaur)**

Triceratops

Despite its fierce appearance, *Triceratops* was a peaceful animal that roamed North America, feeding on plants. It was the largest and heaviest of all the horned dinosaurs and weighed up to 11 tonnes, twice as much as an elephant. Its massive horns would have scared off most enemies.

SIZE:
9 m long

GROUP:
**Ceratopian
(horned dinosaur)**

Styracosaurus

SIZE:
5 m long

GROUP:
**Ceratopian
(horned dinosaur)**

This spectacular dinosaur had a huge, straight horn on its snout and a remarkable bony neck frill, with long spikes arranged around its top. With these weapons, *Styracosaurus* could certainly have defended itself well. Charging head-down, rhinoceros style, at an attacking predator, its great nose horn could have torn into its enemy's flesh while the neck frill gave protection from sharp teeth.

Dromaeosaurus

By hunting in packs, this agile predator could attack and kill prey much larger than itself. It had powerful jaws and sharp fangs, and a large killing claw on each foot with which it could tear into the thick skin of its victims.

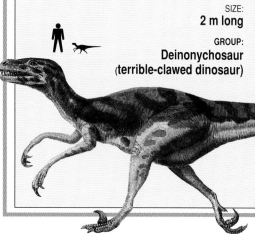

SIZE:
2 m long

GROUP:
**Deinonychosaur
(terrible-clawed dinosaur)**

Lambeosaurus

SIZE:
9 m long

GROUP:
**Ornithopod
(bird-foot dinosaur)**

Lambeosaurus could have moved on all fours or on two legs. It fed on plants and its long, flexible neck may have allowed it to gather food from a wide area without having to move too often. It had two structures on its head—a tall hollow crest and a rear-pointing bony spike.

Ankylosaurus

SIZE:
up to 10 m long

GROUP:
**Ankylosaur
(armoured dinosaur)**

The body of this massive creature was covered with bony, oval plates set into thick, leathery skin. Rows of spikes crossed its body and tail, which ended in a bony club. When attacked, *Ankylosaurus* would probably have stood its ground, protected by its armour. But if the attacker got too near, it might have received a heavy blow from this "living tank's" clubbed tail.

Torosaurus

Torosaurus had the largest head of any known land animal. A huge neck frill rose from the back of its head and three great horns pointed forwards. Its body, too, was large and heavy and its legs stout enough to support its 9-tonne weight. *Torosaurus* led a peaceful life, feeding on plants—few predators would have risked attacking such a fierce looking creature.

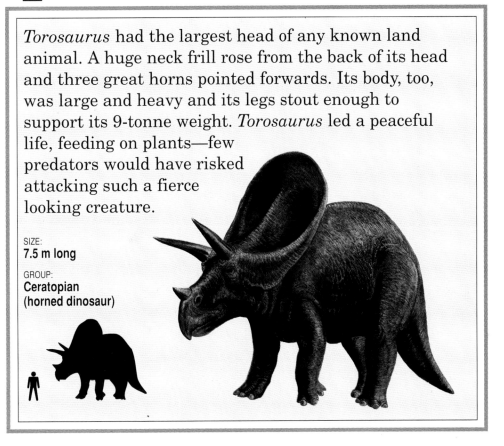

SIZE:
7.5 m long

GROUP:
**Ceratopian
(horned dinosaur)**

93

INDEX

94

Further Reading

Benton, Michael
On the Trail of the Dinosaurs. Kingfisher Books, 1989
Dinosaurs—an A-Z Guide. Kingfisher Books, 1988

Lambert, David/Diagram Group
Collins Guide to Dinosaurs. Collins, 1983
Dinosaur Data Book. Facts on File, 1989

Norman, David and Milner, Angela
Dinosaur. Dorling Kindersley, 1989

Norman, David
Dinosaur! Boxtree 1991
The Illustrated Encyclopedia of Dinosaurs. Salamander Books, 1985

Parker, Steve
Dinosaurs and how they lived. Dorling Kindersley, 1988

Thomas, Barry
The Evolution of Plants and Flowers. Eurobook, 1981

Wellnhofer, Peter
The Illustrated Encyclopedia of Pterosaurs. Salamander Books, 1991

Whitfield, Philip
Why did the dinosaurs disappear? Viking, 1991

Acknowledgements

Illustration credits
Steve Kirk (panoramas on pages 12-13, 30-31, 42-43, 58-59, 70-71 and all catalogue pages)

Mark Iley (pages 22-23, 38-39, 52-53, 66-67, 80-81, 88-89)

Vana Haggarty (line diagram on page 9)

The Publishers would like to thank Dr David Norman of the Sedgwick Museum, Cambridge, England, and Professor Barry Cox of King's College, University of London, for their invaluable advice on the text. We would also like to thank David Whelan and Louise Ellul for computer assistance.